Mountain Biking
Helena

WILL HARMON

FALCON® Helena, Montana

A FALCON GUIDE ®

Falcon® Publishing is continually expanding its list of recreation guidebooks. All books include detailed descriptions, accurate maps, and all the
information necessary for enjoyable trips. You can order extra copies of
this book and get information and prices for other Falcon guidebooks by
writing Falcon Press, P.O. Box 1718, Helena, MT 59624 or calling toll-free 1-
800-582-2665. Also, please ask for a free copy of our current catalog.
Visit our web site at http://www.falconguide.com

Library of Congress Cataloging-in-Publication Data
Harmon, Will.
    Mountain biking Helena / Will Harmon.
        p.   cm.
    "A Falcon guide"—T.p. verso.
    ISBN 1-56044-597-1 (pbk.)
    1. All terrain cycling—Montana—Helena—Guidebooks. 2. Trails—
Montana—Helena—Guidebooks. 3. Helena (Mont.)—Guidebooks.
I. Title
GV1045.5.M762H453 1998
917.86'615—dc21
                                                    97-50156
                                                    CIP

CAUTION
Outdoor recreational activities are by their very nature potentially
hazardous. All participants in such activities must assume the responsibility
for their own actions and safety. The information contained in this
guidebook cannot replace sound judgment and good decision-making
skills, which help reduce the risk exposure, nor does the scope of this book
allow for disclosure of all the potential hazards and risks involved in such
activities.

    Learn as much as possible about the outdoor recreational activities in
which you participate, prepare for the unexpected, and be cautious. The
reward will be a safer and more enjoyable experience.

 Text pages printed on recycled paper.

Contents

Acknowledgments

When you write a book about the place you call home, nearly every neighbor and friend can lay claim to helping in one way or another. Thanks to all those who offered support and encouragement. A handful of people had a more direct influence on the text.

Thanks to Rae Ellen Lee and David Payne at the Helena National Forest for reviewing the work in progress and suggesting a number of rides.

Tom Muri and Jim Barnes also reviewed the manuscript, with a sprocket rocketeer's perspective. Tom and his son Pat accompanied me on several rides, and they added the Little Blackfoot Meadows Loop ride to the book. Thanks for your enthusiasm!

Lots of folks have suggested good rides or interesting route variations over the years. When you meet them on the trail, say hello to Cathy Bakeberg, Simon and Greta Elston, Steve Frankino, Eric Grove, Tom and Jeanann Kirk, Brad Lancaster, Emmett Purcell, Randy Roch, Ken Saunders, Ralph Schmoltz, Mark Shapley, and Dan and Jan Wirak.

Finally, a tip of the helmet to Noelle Sullivan for her careful editing and to Randall Green and the team at Falcon Publishing for sponsoring another summer on the trails.

MAP LEGEND

∿	Trail	🅛 37 →	Trailhead
∿	Unimproved Road	🅛 37	Route Marker
∿	Paved Road	X ⛰	Elevation/Peak
∿	Gravel Road	15	Interstate
∿	Interstate	12	U.S. Highway
∿	Wilderness Boundary	200	State Highway/County Road
∿	Waterway	88	Forest Road
	Lake/Reservoir	●—●	Gate
∿∿∿	Cliff	■	Building
▲	Camping	‿ ⌒	Pass
N ↑ Scale/Compass		╫╫╫╫╫╫	Railroad
		⌣⌣	Bridge
		✕	Mine Site
		⊙	Radio Tower

```
0    1    2    3
▮▮▯▯▮▮▮▯▯▮
     MILES
```

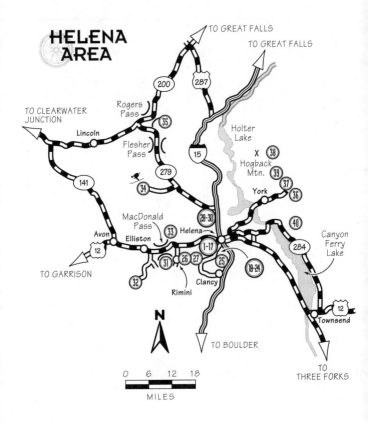

HELENA AREA

TO GREAT FALLS

TO GREAT FALLS

TO CLEARWATER JUNCTION

Rogers Pass

200

287

35

Lincoln

Flesher Pass

15

Holter Lake

X
Hogback Mtn.

38

39

37

36

141

279

34

York

40

MacDonald Pass

33

Helena

284

Canyon Ferry Lake

Avon

Elliston

1-17

32

31

26

27

25

10-24

12

TO GARRISON

Rimini

Clancy

TO BOULDER

12

Townsend

N

0   6   12   18

MILES

TO THREE FORKS

vii

USGS Topo Map Index

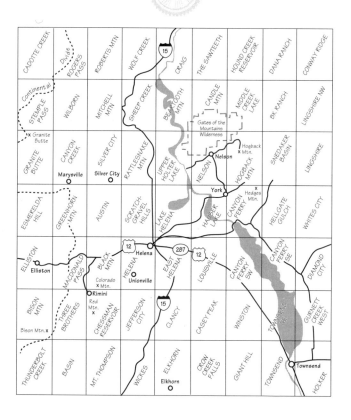

Get Ready to CRANK!

Where to ride? It's a quandary that faces every mountain biker, beginner or expert, local or expatriate.

If you're new to the area, where do you start? If you're a long-time local, how do you avoid riding the same old trails week after week? And how do you find new terrain that's challenging but not overwhelming, or an easier ride for when your not-so-serious buddies want to come along?

Welcome to *Mountain Biking Helena*. Here are forty rides ranging from easy road routes to smooth singletrack to bravado-busting boulder fields. The rides are described in plain language, with accurate distances and ratings for physical and technical difficulty. Each ride description offers a wealth of detailed information that's easy to read from an armchair or use on the trail.

Our aim here is threefold: to help you choose a ride that's appropriate for your fitness and skill level; to make it easy to find the trailhead; and to help you complete the ride safely, without getting lost. Take care of these basics and fun is bound to break loose.

Helena's Hills: What to Expect

The rides in this book cover a widely varied terrain. But most of the rides are mountainous and that means two things: they are steep and rough, and weather can be unpredictable and, at times, severe.

Mountain terrain requires preparedness. Get in good shape before you attempt any of these rides, and know your limits. Keep your bike running smoothly with frequent cleaning and maintenance. Do a quick check before each ride to make sure that tires, rims, brakes, handlebars, seat, shifters, derailleurs, and chain all survived the last ride intact and are functioning properly.

Many of Helena's rides feature extremely steep climbs. Most local riders use a 24- or 22-tooth inner chainring up front, matched to a 32-tooth large cog on the rear sprocket. Even 20-tooth chainrings are not uncommon.

Always carry at least one water bottle (and don't forget to fill it). Snacks, such as fruit or sports energy bars, will help keep your mighty thighs cranking for many hours. Dress for the weather and pack a wind- and water-proof jacket whenever there's any doubt of clear skies. Don't forget sunglasses, sunscreen, lip balm, and insect repellent, as needed.

I tend to go light on tools, but a pump and tube patch kit can save you from a long walk or, on longer rides, a night out. It also helps to carry one or two allen wrenches for tightening or adjusting seat posts, handlebars, chainrings, pedals, brake posts, and other components. Some folks aren't comfortable unless they bring twenty pounds of tools; you can hear them jangling up the trail, but they rarely get stranded by mechanical problems.

Cycling gloves are essential safety equipment—saving hands from cuts and bruises from falls or encroaching branches and rocks. They also improve your grip and comfort on the handlebars. And always wear a helmet: it can save your life.

This book is designed for carrying along in a jersey pocket or bike bag, and the maps and ride descriptions will help anyone unfamiliar with the trails. For more a detailed picture of the terrain (ride routes are not always shown) scan a U.S. Geological Survey topographic map beforehand. The correct maps are listed in the at-a-glance information for each ride.

Climate

Helena's **weather** spans the North American gamut, and is particularly extreme in the surrounding mountains. Snow can fall any day of the year, but summer highs may top 100 degrees F. In general, higher elevations are cooler (by as much as 10 degrees for every 1,000 feet gained) and windier. If you are driving to a trailhead, play it safe and take a variety of clothes in the car to match the variable weather you may encounter.

Most of the good off-road riding in the Helena vicinity happens from May through October. Some trails, particularly at higher elevations, have shorter seasons running from late June through September. (Bear in mind that hunting seasons in some areas may overlap prime pedaling times. For specific dates check with the Montana Department of Fish, Wildlife and Parks; see Appendix B.)

At any time of year rain or snow can turn trails to gumbo for days afterward. Please stay off wet, muddy trails. The risk of soil damage and erosion is simply too great.

In general, trails on Mount Helena's lower west end and in the Scratchgravel Hills (see Rides 5–8 and 29–31) open and dry out earlier than other area trails. In some years these routes are bare and rideable even in winter. Be aware, however, that even a brief rain or minor snowmelt can soften soils and leave trails vulnerable to erosion. Remember, a single bike tire can form a rut that channels runoff on the trail. Water eats at the rut and widens it into an erosion gully that can wipe out that route. Ruts also cause an erosion of public acceptance of bikes on trails. Preventing both types of erosion is essential for preserving access for all mountain bikers.

The yearly number of rainy or snowy days tends to increase the closer you go to the Continental Divide. Many trails west or on top of the divide are often muddy, limiting good riding to eight to ten weeks during the heart of summer.

In general, however, the local climate is semi-arid. Most of Helena's trails drain well, and hard-packed tread sprinkled with bedrock is the norm. Consequently, many local riders prefer clipless pedals over open-cage pedals with toe clips. Clipless pedals and cleated shoes offer better power and leverage when climbing Helena's steep slopes, and there's little risk of mud clogging a pedal.

In winter, most Helena bikers limit their riding to commutes around town or an occasional foray onto frozen jeep roads in the Scratchgravel Hills. In dry years, trails in the South Hills may remain bare and rideable through November and can open again as early as March. But again, please be patient and stay off muddy trails, to avoid erosion and trail damage.

Rules of the Trail

If every mountain biker always yielded the right-of-way, stayed on the trail, avoided wet or muddy trails, never cut switchbacks, never skidded, always rode in control, showed respect for other trail users, and carried out every last scrap of what was carried in (candy wrappers and bike-part debris included)—in short, *did the right thing*—then we wouldn't need a list of rules governing our behavior.

Fact is, most mountain bikers are conscientious and are trying to do right. Most of us *own* that integrity. (No one becomes good at something as demanding and painful as grunting up sheer mountainsides by cheating.) Most of us don't need rules, but we do need knowledge. What exactly *is* the right thing to do?

Here are some guidelines—I like to think of them as reminders—reprinted by permission from the International Mountain Bicycling Association (IMBA). The basic theme here is reducing or eliminating impact on the land and water, the plant and wildlife inhabitants, and other backcountry visitors and trail users. Ride with respect.

IMBA Rules of the Trail

Thousands of miles of dirt trails have been closed to mountain bicyclists. The irresponsible riding habits of a few riders have been a factor in the closure. Do your part to maintain trail access by observing the following rules of the trail, formulated by the International Mountain Bicycling Association (IMBA). IMBA's mission is to promote environmentally sound and socially responsible mountain biking.

1. Ride on open trails only. Respect trail and road closures (ask if not sure), avoid possible trespass on private land, and obtain permits and authorization as required. Federal and state wilderness areas are closed to cycling. The way you ride will influence trail management decisions and policies.

2. Leave no trace. Be sensitive to the dirt beneath you. Even on open (legal) trails, you should not ride under conditions where you will leave evidence of your passing, such as on certain soils after a rain. Recognize different types of soil and trail construction; practice low-impact cycling. This also means staying on existing trails and not creating any new ones. Be sure to pack out at least as much as you pack in.

3. Control your bicycle! Inattention for even a second can cause problems. Obey all bicycle speed regulations and recommendations.

4. Always yield trail. Make known your approach well in advance. A friendly greeting (or bell) is considerate and works well; don't startle others. Show your respect when passing by, slowing to a walking pace or even stopping. Anticipate other trail users around corners or in blind spots.

5. Never spook animals. All animals are startled by an unannounced approach, a sudden movement, or a loud noise. This can be dangerous for you, others, and the animals. Give animals extra room and time to adjust to you. When passing horses use special care and follow directions from the horseback riders (ask if uncertain). Running cattle and disturbing wildlife is a serious offense. Leave gates as you found them, or as marked.

6. Plan ahead. Know your equipment, your ability, and the area in which you are riding—and prepare accordingly. Be self-sufficient at all times, keep your equipment in good repair, and carry necessary supplies for changes in weather or other conditions. A well-executed trip is a satisfaction to you and not a burden or offense to others. Always wear a helmet.

Keep trails open by setting a good example of environmentally sound and socially responsible off-road cycling.

How to Use this Guide

Mountain Biking Helena describes forty mountain bike rides in their entirety. (A handful of other local routes are mentioned briefly in Appendix A.) Many of the featured rides are loops, beginning and ending at the same point but coming and going on different trails. Loops are by far the most popular type of ride, and Helenans are lucky to have so many so close to home.

Be forewarned, however: the difficulty of a loop ride may change dramatically depending on which direction you ride around the loop. If you are unfamiliar with the rides in this book, try them first as described here. The directions follow the path of least resistance (which does not necessarily mean "easy"). After you've been over the terrain, you can determine whether a given loop would be fun—or even feasible—in the reverse direction.

Portions of some rides follow gravel and even paved roads, and a few rides never wander off road. Purists may wince at road rides in a book about mountain biking, but these are special rides. They offer a chance to enjoy mountain scenery and fresh air while covering easier, non-technical terrain for people new to the sport. They can also be used by hard-core riders on "active rest" days or when higher elevation trails are closed by mud or snow.

Each ride description in this book follows the same format:

Number and Name of the Ride: Rides are cross-referenced by number throughout this book. In many cases, parts of rides or entire routes can be linked to other rides for longer trips or variations on a standard route. These opportunities are noted, followed by "see Ride(s) #."

For the names of rides I relied on official names of trails, roads, and natural features as shown on national forest and U.S. Geological Survey maps. In some cases deference was given to long-term local custom, as in "Rodney Ridge," which is not labeled on most maps.

Location: The general whereabouts of the ride; distance and direction from Helena.

Distance: The length of the ride in miles, given as a loop, one way, or round trip.

Time: An estimate of how long it takes to complete the ride (for example, 1 to 2 hours). *The time listed is the actual riding time and does not include rest stops.* Strong, skilled riders may be able to do a given ride in less than the estimated time, and other riders may take considerably longer. Also bear in mind that severe weather, changes in trail conditions, or mechanical problems may prolong a ride.

Tread: The type of road or trail—paved road, gravel road, dirt road or jeep track, doubletrack, ATV-width singletrack, or singletrack.

Aerobic level: The level of physical effort required to complete the ride, rated as easy, moderate, or strenuous. (See the explanation of the rating systems on pages 11 and 12.)

Technical difficulty: The level of bike handling skills needed to complete the ride upright and in one piece. Technical difficulty is rated on a scale from 1 to 5, with 1 being the easiest. (See the explanation of the rating systems on pages 13 and 14.)

Hazards: A list of dangers that may be encountered on a ride, including traffic, weather, trail obstacles and conditions, risky stream crossings, difficult route-finding, and other perils. Remember that conditions may change at any time. Be alert for storms, new fences, downfall, missing trail signs, and mechanical failure. Fatigue, heat, cold, and/or dehydration may impair judgment. Always wear a helmet and other safety equipment.

Ride in control at all times.

Highlights: Special features or qualities that make a ride worth doing (as if we needed an excuse!) such as scenery, fun singletrack, access to other routes, or chances to see wildlife.

Land status: A list of managing agencies or land owners. Most of the rides in this book are on a combination of private property, Helena National Forest, and lands administered by the Bureau of Land Management. Some rides also cross portions of state or municipal lands. More and more trails on private land are being closed to the public, and possible restrictions are noted here for each ride. See page 15 for more information on public access to private lands. Respect the land, regardless of who owns it. See Appendix B for a list of local addresses for land-managing agencies.

Maps: A list of available maps. The Helena National Forest visitors' map (scaled at 1:126,720) affords a good overview of travel routes in the region. USGS topographic maps in the 7.5-minute quad series provide a close-up look at terrain. Many routes are shown on official maps.

Access: How to find the trailhead or the start of the ride. Some rides can be pedaled right from town; for others it's best to drive to the trailhead.

The ride: A mile-by-mile list of key points—landmarks, notable climbs and descents, stream crossings, obstacles, hazards, major turns, and junctions—along the ride. All distances were measured to the tenth of a mile with a cyclo-computer (a bike-mounted odometer). Terrain, riding technique, and even tire pressure can affect odometer readings, so treat all mileages as estimates.

Finally, one last reminder that the real world is changing all the time: the information presented here is as accurate and up-to-date as possible, but there are no guarantees in the mountains. You alone are responsible for your safety and for the choices you make on the trail.

If you do find an error or omission in this book, or a new and noteworthy change in the field, we'd like to hear from you. Please write to Falcon Publishing, P.O. Box 1718, Helena, MT 59624.

Rating the Rides—One Person's Pain is Another's Pleasure

One of the first lessons learned by most mountain bikers is to not trust their friends' accounts of how easy or difficult a given ride may be.

"Where ya wanna ride today?"

"Let's do 'The Wall', dudes—it's gnarly in the middle, but even my grandma could fly up that last hill, and the view is way cool."

If you don't read between the lines, only painful experience will tell you that granny won the pro-elite class in last weekend's hillclimb race and "the view" is over the handlebars from the lip of a thousand-foot drop on that fun little gnarly stretch.

So how do you know what you're getting into, before it's too late?

Don't always listen to your friends, but do read this book. *Falcon mountain biking* guides rate each ride for two types of difficulty: the *physical effort* required to pedal the distance, and the level of *bike-handling skills* needed to stay upright and make it home in one piece. We call these **aerobic level** and **technical difficulty**. The following sections explain what the various ratings mean in plain, specific language.

An elevation profile accompanies each ride description to help you determine how easy or hard the ride is. Also weigh other factors, such as elevation above sea level, total trip distance, weather and wind, and current trail conditions.

Aerobic Level Ratings

Bicycling is often touted as a relaxing, low-impact, relatively easy way to burn excess calories and maintain a healthy heart and lungs. Mountain biking tends to pack a little more work (and excitement) into the routine.

Fat tires and soft or rough trails increase the rolling resistance, so it takes more effort to push those wheels around. Unpaved or off-road hills tend to be steeper than grades measured and tarred by the highway department. When we use the word *steep*, we mean a sweat-inducing, oxygen-sucking, lactose-building climb. If it's followed by an exclamation point—steep (!)—expect some honest pain on the way up (and maybe for days afterward). Expect to breathe hard and sweat some, probably a lot.

Pedaling around town is a good start, but it won't fully prepare you for the workout offered by most of the rides in this book. If you're unsure of your level of fitness, see a doctor for a physical exam before tackling any of the rides included here. And if you're riding to get back in shape or just for the fun of it, take it easy. Walk or rest if need be. Start with short rides and add on miles gradually.

Here's how we rate the exertion level for terrain covered in this book:

Easy: Flat or gently rolling terrain. No steep sections or prolonged climbs. Most riders cruise in the big chainrings up front on "easy" terrain.

Moderate: Some hills. Climbs may be short and fairly steep or long and gradual. Most riders shift into their middle chainrings up front on "moderate" terrain.

Strenuous: Frequent or prolonged climbs steep enough to require riding in the smallest chainring up front, probably in the lowest gear. "Strenuous" terrain requires a high level of aerobic fitness, power, and endurance (typically acquired through many hours of riding and proper training). Less fit riders may need to walk.

Many rides are mostly easy and moderate but may have short strenuous sections. Other rides are mostly strenuous and should be attempted only after a complete medical checkup and implant of a second heart, preferably a *big* one yanked from the chest of last year's Tour de France winner. Also be aware that flailing through a highly technical section can be exhausting even on the flats. Good riding skills and a relaxed stance on the bike save energy.

Finally, any ride can be strenuous if you ride it hard and fast. Conversely, the pain of a lung-burning climb grows easier to tolerate as your fitness level improves. Learn to pace yourself and remember to schedule easy rides and rest days into your calendar.

Elevation Graphs

An elevation profile accompanies each ride description. Here the ups and downs of the route are graphed on a grid of elevation (in feet above sea level) on the left and miles pedaled across the bottom. Route surface conditions (see map legend), and technical levels are shown as well.

Note that these graphs are compressed to fit on the page. The actual

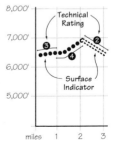

slopes are not as steep as the lines drawn on the graphs, even though it may feel that way. Also, some short dips and climbs are too small to show up on the graphs. Any major grade change, however, will be mentioned in the ride description.

Technical Difficulty Ratings

While you're pushing up that steep, strenuous slope, wondering how much farther you can go before your lungs prolapse and billow out of your mouth like an air bag in a desperate gasp for oxygen, remember that the dry heaves aren't the only hurdle on the way to the top of the mountain. There's also that tree across the trail, or the sideslope full of ball bearing-sized pebbles, or the place where the trail disappears except for faint bits of rubber clinging to the smooth, sheer wall of limestone straight ahead.

Mountain bikes will roll over or through an amazing array of life's little challenges, but sometimes we have to help—or at least close our eyes and hang on. As a last resort, some riders get off their bikes and walk—get this—*before* they flip over the handlebars. These folks have no sense of adventure. The rest of us hop onto our bikes with only the dimmest inkling of what lies ahead. Later we brag about the "ride to hell" (leaving out the part about carrying our bikes half the distance because hell has some highly technical terrain).

No more. The technical difficulty ratings in this book help take the worst surprises out of backcountry rides. In the privacy of your own home you can make an honest appraisal of your bike handling skills, then find rides in these pages that are within your ability.

We rate technical difficulty on a scale from 1 to 5, from easiest to most difficult. We tried to make the ratings as objective as possible by considering the type of obstacles and the frequency of occurrence. The same standards were applied consistently through all the rides in this book.

We've also added plus (+) and minus (-) symbols to cover gray areas between given levels of difficulty: a 4+ obstacle is harder than a 4, but easier than a -5. A stretch of trail rated as 5+ would be unrideable by all but the most skilled (or luckiest) riders.

Here are the five levels defined:

Level 1: Smooth tread; road or doubletrack with no obstacles, ruts, or steeps. Requires basic bike riding skills.

Level 2: Mostly smooth tread; wide, well-groomed singletrack or road/doubletrack with minor ruts or loose gravel or sand.

Level 3: Irregular tread with some rough sections; single or doubletrack with obvious route choices and some steep sections. Occasional obstacles may include small rocks, roots, water bars, ruts, loose gravel or sand, and sharp turns or broad, open switchbacks.

Level 4: Rough tread with few smooth places; singletrack or rough doubletrack with limited route choices and steep sections, some with obstacles. Obstacles are numerous and varied, including rocks, roots, branches, ruts, sidehills, narrow tread, loose gravel or sand, and switchbacks.

Level 5: Continuously broken, rocky, root-infested, or trenched tread; singletrack or extremely rough doubletrack with few route choices and frequent, sudden, or severe changes in gradient. Some slopes are so steep that wheels lift off the ground; obstacles are nearly continuous and may include boulders, logs, water, large holes, deep ruts, ledges, piles of loose gravel, steep sidehills, encroaching trees, and tight switchbacks.

Again, most of the rides in this book cover varied terrain, with an ever-changing degree of technical difficulty. Some trails run smooth with only occasional obstacles, and other trails are seemingly all obstacle. The path of least resistance is where you find it. In general, most obstacles are more challenging if you encounter them while climbing than while descending. On the other hand, in heavy surf (e.g., boulder fields, tangles of downfall, cliffs), fear plays a larger role when facing downhill.

Realize, too, that different riders have different strengths and weaknesses. Some folks can scramble over logs and boulders without a grunt, but they crash head over heels on every switchback turn. Some fly off the steepest drops and others freeze. Some riders climb like the wind and others just blow . . . and walk.

The key to overcoming "technical difficulties" is practice: keep trying. Follow a rider who makes it look easy, and don't hesitate to ask for constructive criticism. Try shifting your weight (good riders move a lot, front to back, side to side, and up and down) and experimenting with balance and momentum. Find a smooth patch of lawn and practice riding as slowly as possible, even balancing at a standstill in a "track stand" (described in the Glossary). This will give you more confidence—and more time to recover or bail out—the next time the trail rears up and bites.

Posted: No Trespassing!

Helena is lucky to have some of the best mountain biking in Montana right out its back door. Mount Ascension, Rodney Ridge, Squaw Gulch, and Mount Helena Ridge are home to a maze of classic double- and singletrack rides all within a bunny hop of downtown.

But this maze features more than its share of dead ends—"no trespassing" signs, trees splashed with orange paint, and barbed-wire fences strung across trails. Sadly, new dead ends crop up every season, closing once-popular trails and, in some cases, blocking access to public lands beyond.

A glance at the Helena National Forest Visitor Map reveals the scope of the problem. If the trails are a maze, the lands they cross are a jigsaw puzzle of public and private ownership. Take out the private pieces of the puzzle and the maze cannot be unriddled from start to finish.

Similar situations are also found in the Scratchgravel Hills, along sections of the Continental Divide, in the North Hills, and in the Big Belt and Elkhorn mountains.

Many of the private holdings are old mining claims—strips and odd-shaped scraps that ignore topography in favor of following hoped-for veins of wealth below ground. Today these parcels are prospected for their value as home sites, and the owners are growing ever more cautious about who goes traipsing across their investments. Where people have recently built homes, they typically close old trails to keep the public off their new backyards. That's their prerogative: public access to private land is a privilege, not a right. We should thank the many landowners who have allowed access for so many years.

But what the current trend means to us mountain bikers (and hikers, runners, and horseback riders) is that our local trail network is shrinking. Mount Ascension has long been private property, but only since 1990 have its trails been posted against trespassing. The private lands surrounding Rodney Ridge and Squaw Gulch have seen more new fence during the last five years than in the previous fifty. And even Mount Helena, which is a city park, can claim only one designated public trailhead (the Adams Street parking lot).

In fact, twenty of the forty rides described in this book cross private property. As of this writing, public access on these trails is doubtful at best. No legal rights-of-way or recreation easements are currently in place. Some landowners have begun to hint that access may soon be restricted (by putting a gate or debris across a trail but not posting signs or orange paint). In short, it's the reader's responsibility to determine whether the trails—even those described on the following pages—are open or not.

So why include such rides in this book? Why not focus more on trails farther from town, on national forest and Bureau of Land Management lands? In part, it's because even those federal lands are quilted with private property. Public access to Forest Service and BLM trails is not necessarily more secure. But the rides described in this book are here also because there is hope. We still have a chance to keep most of these trails open.

In a few cases landowners have informally allowed access as long as trail users don't cause any problems. Other landowners grant use of the trails on an individual basis when cyclists ask permission ahead of time. And more widespread efforts are being made to acquire easements and rights-of-way (or even to buy land outright) by several conservation groups based in Helena. Open Space Helena hopes to raise funds through a bond issue for buying land in and around town to set aside for views and recreation. The Prickly Pear Land Trust is working to secure lands and access in the Scratchgravel Hills and throughout the South Hills, both to preserve plant and wildlife habitat and to provide recreational opportunities. The trust's first land purchase was a chunk of Rodney Ridge that allows access to the historic Waterline Trail. Another group, Plan Helena, hopes to address the problem by building public support for more enlightened land-use planning and management. For more information on these and other groups, see the addresses in Appendix B.

In the meantime, all trail users should follow a few rules of common courtesy (and Montana law).
•Ask permission first to enter or cross private property. Check at local bike shops or the County Assessor's Office (see Appendix B) for land ownership information.

•Familiarize yourself with Montana trespass law, particularly section 46-6-201 of the Montana Code Annotated. According to the law, you can enter private land only with explicit permission from the landowner or if the land is not posted against trespass. The posting requirements are simple: written notice (a sign) or 50 square inches of orange paint on a post, structure, or natural object. If property is posted, no one is allowed access without permission from the landowner. If land is not posted, anyone can legally enter, but it's still best to ask permission first.

•Respect all property, private or public. Leave all gates as you find them. Do not damage fences or other facilities, and avoid spooking livestock.

•Strive to be inconspicuous. Ride quietly and in small groups. Prevent erosion: do not skid or ride when trails are wet and muddy. Stay on designated trails and roads. Check your bike and clothing for seeds and weeds to prevent the spread of noxious plants. Knapweed and toadflax are common around Helena; both are easily snagged in chains and pedals. Do not litter.

•Wear a helmet and ride in control at all times. Landowners and managers are less skittish about mountain bikers when we take responsibility for our own safety. If you do get hurt, don't blame the landowner.

•If you meet the landowner while on the property, be friendly and honest. You are an ambassador for all riders who follow. Some landowners see mountain bikers as a liability risk—"What if a biker crashes and gets hurt on my land? Will he or she sue me?" You can reassure them by taking time to talk with them as any reasonable person would (but please don't show off your chainring scars and missing teeth). Some folks know about the Montana recreation access law (70-16-302, MCA), which limits the liability of landowners who allow free use of their property for recreation. Mention this if it seems appropriate to the conversation. And take every opportunity to thank the landowner for allowing access to his or her property.

Finally, consider joining one of the local groups working to preserve trails and land access. Chip in when they hold a work day to repair and maintain trails, pull weeds, or pick up trash. Pay membership dues in lieu of joining a health club, then get your workout on the trails you've helped protect. Become more involved in helping city and county officials plan and develop local open space opportunities. In short, be an all-around advocate for trails.

1906 Trail—Mount Helena Summit

Location: On the southwest edge of downtown Helena, Mount Helena City Park.

Distance: 1.6 miles one way. Can be used as part of various loop rides ranging from 3.1 to 14 miles.

Time: 20 to 50 minutes up, 15 minutes down.

Tread: 1.6 miles on singletrack.

Aerobic level: Strenuous—for strong riders only.

Technical difficulty: Mostly 3 to 3+ for experienced singletrack riders. Water bars are numerous at the start and near the summit. These are 3+. Two rock steps above the junction with the West End Trail rate a 5 going up and a 4+ coming down. The final pitch to the summit features a few solid 5 moves.

Hazards: Off-angled water bars (slick, especially when wet); heavy trail use. CAUTION: Ride in control at all times and always yield the right-of-way to hikers and runners. When riding

•1906 Trail–
Mount Helena Summit

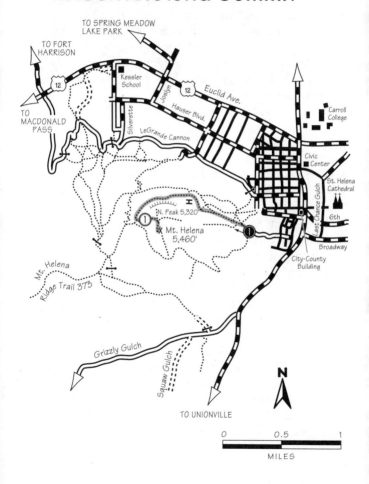

downhill, yield to uphill cyclists. Also, watch for unleashed dogs.

Highlights: A lung-busting climb, the 1906 Trail is the least technically difficult approach to the summit of Mount Helena. It offers classic singletrack climbing for strong riders, good views of town, and access to other trails (see Rides 2, 3, and 4), including the Mount Helena Ridge National Recreation Trail (see Rides 11 and 12). The trail was built in 1904, but the erroneous "1906" label has stuck.

Land status: Mount Helena City Park.

Maps: A Mount Helena Park map showing trails is available at the Lewis and Clark County Library and sometimes on the information rack by the Park Avenue door of the City-County Building. USGS Helena.

Access: From the City-County Building on Park Avenue in downtown Helena, pedal one block west on Clarke Street, then turn left (south) on Benton Avenue and go two blocks. Turn right on Adams Street and climb hard two blocks to Howie. Continue straight on Adams, which turns to dirt here. Go right on a footpath around the gate and continue 0.2 mile uphill to the parking lot at road's end (a total of 0.6 mile from Park Avenue). Odometer readings for the ride begin at the map and information kiosk on the west end of the lot.

To drive to the trailhead, go south on Park Avenue from the City-County Building. After 0.6 mile, turn right onto Carriage Lane (look for a sign for Reeders Village and another for Mount Helena City Park). Go uphill 0.1 mile and turn right onto Village Drive. Continue uphill through the Reeders Village neighborhood. Take the next right and then immediately turn left onto dirt Adams Street. Go 0.1 mile uphill on Adams to the parking lot and trailhead.

The ride:

0.0 Stop at the map kiosk to get oriented and to read park rules regarding trail users, including cyclists. Take a swig of water, then pedal west on the dirt singletrack that leaves from behind the right side of the kiosk.

Just past the chainlink fence a trail cuts right to a picnic table and access trails coming from Holter and Monroe streets. Stay straight on the main trail.

0.1 A cluster of side trails. Two spurs on the right go down to the Holter and Monroe trailheads. On the left, the first trail contours down and south to the Prospect Shafts Trail (Ride 4). The second left is the Powerline Trail, bounding uphill. Ignore all of these side trails and continue climbing on the 1906 Trail. The early going has frequent log water bars and sandy tread, making the initial climb trickier than it should be.

0.2 The Prairie Trail goes right (see Ride 2); stay straight and pump over a short rocky stretch.

0.5 The grade eases slightly and contours across an open slope. The Holter Street Access Trail runs up from the right, and the 1906 Trail swings north below the big, white "H" on the hillside. Watch for runners and cyclists barreling downhill around the next blind curve.

0.6 A side trail drops right 70 yards to the Prairie Trail; stay straight. Grade eases.

0.7 Gear down—if you've got a lower gear you haven't used yet—and suck air for the next 150 yards. This is the steepest sustained pitch of the entire climb.

0.9 Devil's Kitchen—a soot-stained cave—is uphill on the left. It makes a good rest stop for those so inclined. Park your bike well off trail.

1.0 Enjoy an all-too-brief downhill, then resume climbing.

1.2 The grade eases near a junction with the West End Trail

(a link to the Prairie Trail, Ride 2, and the Mount Helena Ridge Trail, Rides 11 and 12) on the right. Lean left and pedal up to a gnarly chunk of bedrock across the trail—a 4+ obstacle—followed by another, toothier chunk—a solid 5 when riding uphill. Aim for the tire-wide slot or scamper over the rocks just left of the slot without falling to the downhill side. From here the trail turns up and over a fat water bar and a root in a twisted switchback, then eases off to a moderate climb on smooth tread. Wiggle through the next set of rocks—a -4 move.

1.4 A blocked shortcut goes right and a side trail climbs left to radio towers and a clifftop perch. Stay straight on the main trail. In 80 yards the Powerline Trail (best suited for hikers) and "H" Trail (closed to all use) split off left. Instead, lean right and climb hard again toward the summit. Claw your way over a series of water bars.

1.5 Puzzle through a narrow, rocky section with few route choices. Most folks shoot for the tire-wide trench against the juniper on the right. Recuperate on the short, flat stretch (stairs go left up to the summit), then punch it over a low rock step to the summit ridge. The trail turns left here, up a nasty rock step (5+) that stops most folks (if the previous rocks haven't). Park your bike here or jam it on up to . . .

1.6 The official summit. Any water left in that bottle? Town looks small way down there . . . why's it spinning? Welcome to 5,460 feet above sea level. The 360-degree views stretch from MacDonald Pass to peaks in the Scapegoat Wilderness west and north, and from the Elkhorns to Mount Baldy in the southern end of the Big Belts south and east. Retrace your tracks back to town, or swing left at the West End junction (see mile 1.2 above) and drop down the Prairie Trail (Ride 2) for a fresh singletrack downhill.

Prairie Trail

Location: In Mount Helena City Park, on the southwest edge of downtown Helena.

Distance: 1.5 miles one way. Can be used as part of various loops ranging from 3.1 to 14 miles.

Time: 20 to 45 minutes up, 10 to 20 minutes down.

Tread: 1.5 miles on singletrack.

Aerobic level: Strenuous with a moderate midsection.

Technical difficulty: Mostly -3. Two series of tight, steep switchbacks are 4+; the bottom-most switchback is a solid 5.

Hazards: Off-angled, rubber water bars (slick, especially when wet) in upper section, heavy trail use. CAUTION: Ride in control at all times and always yield the right-of-way to hikers and runners. When riding downhill, yield to uphill cyclists. Also watch for unleashed dogs. Wait for dry weather—parts of this trail stay muddy longer than other Mount Helena trails.

•Prairie Trail

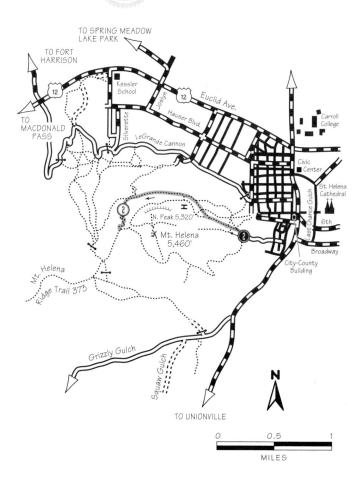

TO SPRING MEADOW LAKE PARK

TO FORT HARRISON

TO MACDONALD PASS

12

Kessler School

Joslyn

12 Euclid Ave.

Hauser Blvd.

Silverette

LeGrande Cannon

Carroll College

Civic Center

St. Helena Cathedral

6th

Last Chance Gulch

Broadway

City-County Building

N. Peak 5,320

Mt. Helena 5,460'

Mt. Helena Ridge Trail 373

Grizzly Gulch

Squaw Gulch

TO UNIONVILLE

N

0   0.5   1

MILES

Highlights: Ridden top to bottom, the Prairie Trail is the most popular downhill on Mount Helena and one of the best sections of smooth, sinuous singletrack in the area. Locals call it "Star Wars," because at speed the trailside trees blur like the stars when Han Solo shifts into hyperspace. Riders with exceptional balance and quick reflexes will enjoy the E-ticket ride. But please ride in control: no skidding (even on tight switchbacks), and always yield to other trail users. Reckless riding will only stir up anti-bike sentiment and could lead to trail restrictions or closures. Try it going up first (as it's described here) to get a taste of the switchbacks. The Prairie Trail also offers access to other trails and a chance of seeing deer, fox, and birds of prey.

Land status: Mount Helena City Park.

Maps: A Mount Helena City park map showing trails is available at the Lewis and Clark County Library. USGS Helena.

Access: From the City-County Building on Park Avenue in downtown Helena drive or pedal west on Clarke Street one block to Benton Avenue. Turn left (south) on Benton and go two blocks. Turn right on Adams Street and climb hard two blocks to Howie. Continue straight on Adams, which turns to dirt here. Go around the gate and continue 0.2 mile uphill to the parking lot at road's end. Odometer readings for the ride begin at the map and information kiosk on the west end of the lot.

The ride:

0.0 Pedal west and uphill on the 1906 Trail (Ride 1), tractoring over frequent, fat water bars.

0.2 Turn left onto the easier grade of the Prairie Trail (a sign sometimes marks this junction).

0.3 The Holter Street Access Trail cuts across the route; continue climbing west on the Prairie Trail.

0.4 The Quarry Trail goes right (connecting to the Holter Access Trail); stay straight.

0.6 Top of initial climb. A 70-yard connecting trail goes left and hard uphill to the 1906 Trail; stay straight and slip into your middle chainring for some downhill fun. The trail alternates between open, grassy slopes with good views of Helena's west end and shady stands of pine and fir. Watch for oncoming traffic.

1.0 Sunset Point. Begin climbing in earnest again, banking uphill and left (fading side trails break right and straight—see Ride 3). The Prairie Trail re-enters the trees and swings right to the first set of switchbacks. There are two turns in the first set and four in the second.

1.1 Bust a move if you think you can squeegee over the root step in this first (and hardest—a full-bore 5) switchback going left.

1.2 Climb hard onto a gentle spur ridge and swing left on an easier grade. Then gear down for the second set of switchbacks. The first turn goes left. Climb hard and swing right, then charge the double switchback—two turns stacked one on top of the other. From here the grade eases and the trail winds through a stand of spindly trees.

1.5 Triangle junction with the West Ridge Trail. Go right to ride the Mount Helena Ridge National Recreation Trail (Rides 11 and 12) or to reach the Early Summer–Seven Sisters Ridge Trail (Ride 8) for a fun route off the mountain. Go left 150 yards to meet the 1906 Trail for access to Mount Helena's summit or a quick descent route.

Ed Eschler's Loop

Location: In Mount Helena City Park, on the southwest edge of Helena's Upper West Side neighborhood.

Distance: 5.7-mile loop.

Time: 30 minutes to 1 hour.

Tread: 0.8 mile on paved road; 2.1 miles on gravel road; 0.9 mile on doubletrack; 1.9 miles on singletrack.

Aerobic level: Moderate, with a somewhat strenuous climb to the Prairie Trail.

Technical difficulty: Mostly -3 to 3+; 1 to 2 on paved and gravel roads.

Hazards: Watch for traffic on all open roads. CAUTION: Ride in control at all times and always yield the right-of-way to hikers and runners. When riding downhill, yield to uphill cyclists. Also watch for unleashed dogs. Wait for dry weather—parts of this trail stay muddy longer than other Mount Helena trails.

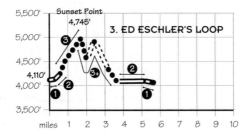

•Ed Eschler's Loop

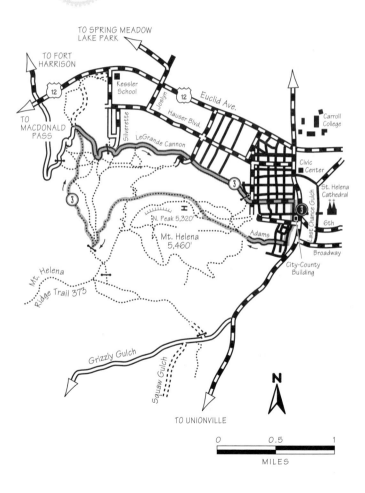

TO SPRING MEADOW
LAKE PARK

TO FORT
HARRISON

12

TO
MACDONALD
PASS

Kessler
School

Joslyn

12

Euclid Ave.

Hauser Blvd.

Silverette

LeGrande Cannon

3

Carroll
College

Civic
Center

St. Helena
Cathedral

Last Chance Gulch

3

6th

N. Peak 5,320'

Mt. Helena
5,460'

Adams

Broadway

Mt. Helena
Ridge Trail 373

City-County
Building

Grizzly Gulch

Squaw Gulch

TO UNIONVILLE

N

0   0.5   1
MILES

Highlights: This is one of the less strenuous routes on Mount Helena, with good views of town, a surprisingly secluded section of wooded trail, and a chance of seeing deer and other wildlife. These features made this loop a favorite of Ed Eschler, a well-liked and respected road and mountain biker and marathon runner who inspired many Helena athletes by competing well into his 60s. After Ed passed away in May 1996, his friends named this loop ride in his honor.

Land status: Mount Helena City Park; private. From mile 1.8 to 3.4 this route crosses private property. During summer 1996 some trails and jeep roads in this area were posted against trespass. Future access remains uncertain.

Maps: USGS Helena; Mount Helena City Park map available at the Lewis and Clark County Library.

Access: Ride this loop from town, starting at the City-County Building on Park Avenue.

The ride:

0.0 From the City-County Building on Park Avenue pedal west on Clarke Street one block to Benton Avenue. Turn left (south) on Benton and go two blocks.

0.2 Turn right on Adams Street and climb hard two blocks to Howie.

0.3 Continue straight on Adams, which turns to dirt here. Go right on a footpath around the gate and pedal hard 0.2 mile uphill to the Mount Helena parking lot at road's end.

0.6 From the trailhead map kiosk pedal west and uphill on the 1906 Trail (Ride 1), tractoring over frequent, fat water bars.

0.8 Turn left onto the easier grade of the Prairie Trail (see

Ride 2); a sign sometimes marks this junction.

1.0 The Holter Street Access Trail cuts across the route; continue climbing west on the Prairie Trail.

1.1 The Quarry Trail goes right (connecting to the Holter Access Trail); stay straight.

1.2 Top of initial climb. A 70-yard connecting trail goes left and hard uphill to the 1906 Trail; stay straight and slip into your middle chainring for some downhill fun. The trail alternates between open, grassy slopes with good views of Helena's west end and shady stands of pine and fir. Watch for oncoming traffic.

1.7 At Sunset Point, the Prairie Trail banks uphill and left and a sign marks the North Side Access Trail, which dives into the trees on the right. Go straight instead on a faint, grassy trail. It forks immediately—veer left and drop west through a thicket of dog-hair fir. Ignore another trail breaking right and downhill.

1.8 Dodge downhill through a more open lodgepole forest with occasional rocks on the tread.

1.9 A spur trail splits left and uphill; stay right and continue the gradual descent.

2.1 Squeeze around a tree on sidesloped tread, then lean right and join the Gully doubletrack. For the fastest route home, turn right and fly downhill 0.7 mile to LeGrande. To stay on Ed's course, turn left and ride uphill through a rock garden.

2.2 Swoop through a quick dip in the track and bear left (uphill) where another doubletrack enters from the right.

2.3 Climb to a cul-de-sac and bear right onto singletrack running west along the fenced boundary of Mount Helena City Park.

2.4 Pedal up to a pass gate in the fence at a small opening in the trees. Turn right and dive downhill onto singletrack lined with trees and often choked with pine cones. This is the Early Summer–Seven Sisters Ridge Trail (Ride 8).

2.5 Bank left and spin up a short grade to regain the ridge proper.

2.6 Ignore the doubletrack that falls away on the right. Instead, bounce down doubletrack going straight north.

2.8 Scramble up a low hump in the ridge, then peel off another fast downhill. Watch for ruts and sidesloped tread.

3.0 After bashing over some toothy bedrock, roll out into a crossroads of sorts. Veer left at about 11 o'clock to stay on the ridge; several other doubletracks drop down either side from here. The trail soon roller-coasters downhill, smoothly at first, then nearly derailing on bedrock across the tread.

3.2 Roll onto a low saddle just above the Early Summer jeep road hillclimb described in Ride 7. Stay on the ridge, climbing briefly on doubletrack going north.

3.3 The tread narrows to singletrack twisting downhill. Watch for limestone fangs.

3.4 The trail bottoms out on LeGrande Cannon Boulevard. Turn right and pedal east. The road curves northeast on a level grade, then beelines east above Helena's Upper West Side neighborhood. Stay on LeGrande, ignoring all side roads (see Ride 5).

5.2 East end closure. Wiggle through the opening on the left end of the guardrail then turn left on paved Holter Street. Grab those brakes and look both ways at all intersections (there are no stop signs) as you careen downhill seven blocks.

5.6 Turn left on Benton Avenue and pedal one block south.

5.7 Roll up to the City-County Building and the end of the loop.

Prospect Shafts Trail

Location: In Mount Helena City Park, on the southwest edge of downtown Helena.

Distance: 1.9 miles.

Time: 25 to 50 minutes up, 20 minutes down.

Tread: 1.9 miles on singletrack.

Aerobic level: Strenuous.

Technical difficulty: 3 to 5+. Sections of tread are rock-bound (plenty of 5; one spot of 5+), others are gravelly and loose. A set of water bars on the steepest leg rates 4+.

Hazards: Rocky sections can jam wheels—be prepared to step out or fall. Off-angled water bars (slick, especially when wet); heavy trail use. CAUTION: Ride in control at all times and always yield to hikers and runners. When riding downhill, yield to uphill cyclists. Watch for unleashed dogs.

Highlights: This is the most technically difficult approach to

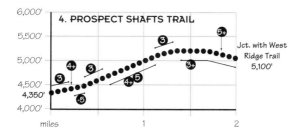

•Prospect Shafts Trail

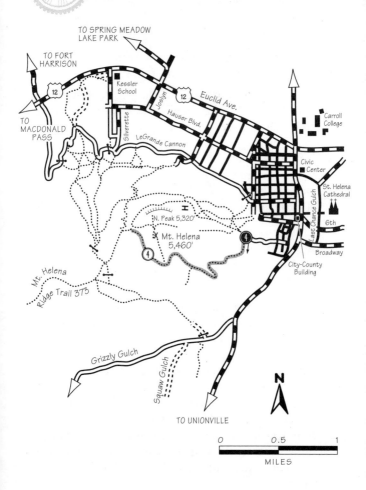

TO SPRING MEADOW
LAKE PARK

TO FORT
HARRISON

12

TO MACDONALD
PASS

Kessler
School

Joslyn

12 Euclid Ave.

Hauser Blvd.

Silverette

LeGrande Cannon

Carroll
College

Civic
Center

St. Helena
Cathedral

Last Chance Gulch

6th

N. Peak 5,320

Mt. Helena
5,460'

4

4

Broadway

City-County
Building

Mt. Helena
Ridge Trail 373

Grizzly Gulch

Squaw Gulch

TO UNIONVILLE

N

0   0.5   1
MILES

the summit of Mount Helena. A rideable line is almost always obvious, but obstacles are varied and occur over long stretches; it's a fun test piece. There's good access to other trails, including the Mount Helena Ridge National Recreation Trail (Ride 11).

Land status: Mount Helena City Park.

Maps: A Mount Helena Park map showing trails is available at the Lewis and Clark County Library. USGS Helena.

Access: From the City-County Building on Park Avenue in downtown Helena drive or pedal west on Clarke Street one block to Benton Avenue. Turn left (south) on Benton and go two blocks. Turn right on Adams Street and climb hard two blocks to Howie. Continue straight on Adams, which turns to dirt here. Go around the gate and continue 0.2 mile uphill to the parking lot at road's end. Odometer readings for the ride begin at the map and information kiosk on the west end of the lot.

The ride:

0.0 Stop at the map kiosk to get oriented and read park rules regarding trail users, including cyclists. Take a swig of water, then pedal south through the parking lot to the singletrack at its south end. A sign marks it as the Prospect Shafts Trail. This is the only Mount Helena Trail that begins on the level. In 30 feet there's a junction; a cross-trail goes right to link with the 1906 Trail and left to Reeder's Village. Stay straight.

0.1 Turn right at a post (unofficial trails go straight and left) and begin a somewhat strenuous climb into the trees. Frequent water bars cross the tread for the next 0.2 mile.

0.3 The trail banks right through the bottom of a small gully, then immediately humps up the other side. A water bar and a set of rocks block the way—aim for the tire-wide gap and pedal hard. It's a 4+ obstacle. Then the trail turns left and skirts a picnic table, climbing through a -5 boulder garden. An unbroken line is hard to find; improvise! Some wag must have put the picnic table here so folks could watch the mountain bike rodeos caused by this rocky stretch.

0.4 Swing down and left through a sharp turn in the gully again. Climb out and into a switchback going right. The steady climb continues on wide, somewhat rocky tread.

0.5 Swing left in a big turn and enjoy mostly smooth tread as the trail contours through the pines.

0.7 The trail breaks out of the trees onto the nose of a ridge and into the wind (on most days—or into full-bore sun on a sweltering July afternoon). A fading singletrack goes left and down; go right instead, staying on the gravelly main track. Tuck in your mental shirttails and get ready for 0.5 mile of technical, strenuous scrambling. The trail winds through scattered trees and fangs of bedrock poking up through the rubble. Expect poor traction, wheel traps, a tight turn or two, and short steeps.

1.0 Cross a rocky slab and set your sights on the crux move just ahead—a mini Rock of Gibraltar across the trail. Some people try to skirt this on the right, but you can ride the rocks themselves. Either angle between them or power straight over their tops . . . but be ready to slam a foot down to prevent a nasty fall. A side trail also splits off left in this section—it dead-ends in about 0.2 mile around the south flank of the mountain.

1.1   The climb steepens on loose gravel. Fat water bars
      angle across the tread, requiring lunges midclimb.
1.2   Turn hard left and ease onto a short level grade. From
      here the trail climbs moderately into a scattering of
      trees.
1.3   A sign marks the Hogback Trail going right and madly
      uphill to the summit. Don't try it unless you enjoy car-
      rying your bike up stairs. Instead, shift into your middle
      chainring (if you haven't already) to prevent chain suck,
      and go straight over two humps of bedrock. This alter-
      nately rocky and smooth leg is known as the Backside
      Trail.
1.6   The trail continues its nearly level contour above some
      cliffy limestone outcrops just off trail.
1.7   Drop into a small swale, dip left, and slow down for
      . . .
1.8   A toothy rock step down. Some diehards ride this 5+
      obstacle, but the crashes can be spectacular (and expen-
      sive). There's no shame in portaging your bike. A sec-
      ond, lesser ledge (a 4+) immediately follows.
1.9   The trail rolls out into a Y junction with the West End
      Trail. The right-hand trail leads uphill 100 yards to the
      1906 Trail (Ride 1) and the summit (in 0.4 mile); the
      left-hand route goes 50 yards to the Prairie Trail (Ride
      2) and the beginning of the Mount Helena Ridge Trail
      (Ride 11).

Most locals prefer riding Prospect Shafts as a challenging
uphill. Going down, it tends to rattle loose pieces of bike and
bone. Downhillers should also be alert for endo-inducing wheel
traps and steps.

LeGrande Cannon Boulevard

Location: On Helena's upper west edge, running from Holter Street to U.S. Highway 12 west.

Distance: 3.2 miles one way.

Time: 15 to 40 minutes, east to west.

Tread: 3.2 miles on gravel road.

Aerobic level: Easy from east to west, but west to east there's a moderate climb.

Technical difficulty: 2.

Hazards: Watch for traffic, potholes, pedestrians, and dogs.

Highlights: Good views of town and Mount Helena; access to west-end trails. A 0.9-mile section of LeGrande (between Silverette Street and the west end) is closed to vehicles—a great place for slow, easy rides, especially with kids.

Land status: Public (City of Helena) and private.

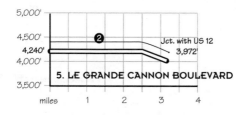

LeGrande Cannon Boulevard

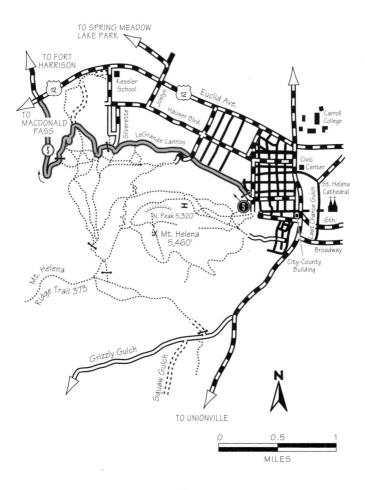

Maps: USGS Helena.

Access: From the City-County Building on Park Avenue, pedal one block west (uphill) on Lawrence. Turn right onto Benton Avenue and go one long block north to Holter Street. Turn left on Holter and climb (moderate to steep) six blocks west to the end of pavement and the beginning of LeGrande Cannon Boulevard.

The ride

0.0 Pedal west on LeGrande, which at the time of this writing was closed to motor vehicles on a section at its east end. Despite its "grand" name, this boulevard feels more like a country back road. It was named in honor of a favored scion of one of Helena's early millionaires (imagine the teasing poor little LeGrande's name inspired in grade school). Enjoy the views north to the Scratchgravel Hills and west to the Continental Divide. Mount Helena looms to the south. Homes line the boulevard on both sides.

0.6 Henderson, a major through street, drops downhill and right to U.S. Highway 12. Stay straight on LeGrande.

0.8 The roadway narrows and most of suburbia's sprawl stays farther down the hill from here on out.

1.1 Private drives on left; stay straight on main road.

1.3 Several jeep tracks climb away to the Gully on the left (see Ride 3). Follow LeGrande as it curves right.

1.4 Silverette Street drops right (0.4 mile) to Hauser Boulevard, a good access/escape point when other sections of LeGrande are muddy. Just ahead a gate blocks vehicle access to the next section of LeGrande. Ride past the gate on the left and keep to the inside lane to avoid pedestrians. From here the ride is more rural, almost remote. Pine trees and steep slopes offer shade, and birds are plentiful.

1.5 Concrete bridge. A singletrack splits left just before the bridge—an alternate route up the Gully. Follow LeGrande as it curves north beneath Jeep, one of the Early Summer Wall hillclimbs (see Ride 7).

1.9 Early Summer–Seven Sisters Ridge Trail crosses road (see Rides 3 and 8).

2.1 Doubletrack goes left to West Bowl hillclimbs where LeGrande makes a sharp right turn. A series of doubletracks here climb a wide, shallow bowl to Early Summer–Seven Sisters Ridge. It's strenuous but short, with a tech rating of 3; be careful in the ruts down low. Continue west on LeGrande, which curves left.

2.3 West-end closure gate. Just beyond the gate the Dozer Direct Trail climbs hard (!) on the left to reach Early Summer–Seven Sisters Ridge Trail in 300 yards. LeGrande swings right. This is a good turnaround spot for riders who want to stay on the flats and avoid traffic. To reach the end of LeGrande, keep pedaling west.

2.5 Hairpin right turn; ranch driveway on left. Begin fast downhill run.

3.2 Junction with US 12 across from the Corner Bar and Broadwater Market. Turn right onto US 12 for the quickest route back to town (about 4.5 miles to the City-County Building). To link up with the Centennial Park–Spring Meadow Trail (Ride 6), cross US 12 and pedal north one block on Williams Street. Turn right at the first gravel road just before the bridge over Tenmile Creek. There's no sign, but this is Broadwater Avenue. Go 0.3 mile east to the old Kessler Brewery. Dogleg right onto pavement and then turn left onto the gravel road that wraps around the northwest end of Spring

Meadow Lake. Ride 0.5 mile and turn right on Country Club Road. Go another 0.4 mile and turn left onto a singletrack that rolls over a hump onto an old railroad bed; this is the Centennial Park bike path (Ride 6).

Centennial Park– Spring Meadow Trail

Location: Between the YMCA/Carroll College and Spring Meadow State Park, paralleling the railroad tracks on Helena's west end.

Distance: 2.3 miles one way.

Time: 15 to 30 minutes one way.

Tread: 2 miles on wide, one-lane sandy bike path; 0.3 mile on roadside singletrack.

Aerobic level: Easy.

Technical difficulty: 2, but watch for pockets of sand and a few bumpy spots.

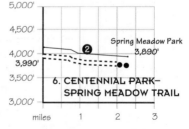

Hazards: Yield to other path users. Stop and watch for traffic at the Benton, Henderson, Joslyn, and Country Club road crossings and also at the garbage transfer station.

43

· Centennial Park–
Spring Meadow Trail

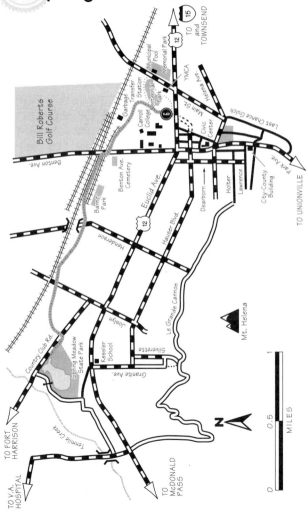

Use care when crossing railroad tracks at Benton Avenue. Sand traps near the west end make steering and pedaling difficult, especially for children.

Highlights: This rails-to-trails bike path provides good off-street riding and access to Centennial, Barney, and Spring Meadow Lake parks. It also showcases the sights, sounds, (and sometimes smells) of Helena's behind-the-scenes infrastructure—not the city's prettiest face, but interesting in its own right.

Land status: City of Helena and State of Montana.

Maps: City map (in the phone book); USGS Helena.

Access: Start from Centennial Park, which includes the softball and soccer fields west of the YMCA and the National Guard Armory at the corner of Lyndale and Main. To bike there from downtown Helena, go to the Civic Center, at the corner of Benton and Neill avenues. Pedal east one block on Neill and turn left on Getchell. Go two blocks north, then turn right on the dirt drive into the Great Northern industrial district (just before Montana Recycling). Trend north (left) and go under the Lyndale overpass to the sandy running track that circles Centennial Park. Turn left and pedal 0.1 mile to a wooden post marking a wider, sandy path that drops away on the left. Start here.

The ride:

0.0   Centennial Park fields. Go north on the bike path as it contours between an old railroad spur and the slopes leading down from hilltop Carroll College.

0.2   Bike path junction. The right-hand path goes 0.2 mile east to rejoin the Centennial Park running trail. Instead, turn left toward the city's garbage transfer station.

0.3 Cross the main transfer station road and head west on the sandy path along an old rail spur. Cross a second road just after the station's entrance booth. CAUTION: Watch for traffic at both crossings.

0.6 The bike path crosses Benton Avenue where railroad tracks also cross. Pedal straight across Benton, then turn right onto the wide asphalt sidewalk before crossing the railroad tracks. Try to keep your wheels at right angles to the tracks so they don't get trapped in the grooves. Coast about 50 yards downhill and cross another set of railroad tracks. Look for wooden posts on the left that marks where the bike path continues west, running between two sets of railroad tracks. An interpretive sign gives the railroading history of this line. Pedal west.

1.0 A wooden post on the left marks a side trail to Barney Park (softball, tennis, basketball, playground, picnic shelter). The main trail continues west.

1.1 Cross a stout wooden bridge (watch for metal posts at either end). Kids enjoy swooping down the concrete spillway into the barrow pit here, but watch for broken glass and other nasty debris. Continue west on the bike path.

1.2 Drop down to Henderson Street. A singletrack splits left (south) for access to Henderson and Hudson streets and adjoining neighborhoods, but the main trail continues west. CAUTION: descend slowly, come to a full stop, and look for traffic both ways before crossing Henderson. Gear down for the short, moderate climb back up to the railroad grade on the other side. Pedal west.

1.7 Cross Joslyn Street.

1.9 Stay to the right around a playground area. Slow down when children are present. Be alert for pockets of sand.

2.0 Ease over an abrupt hump and watch for traffic as you turn right (west) onto paved Country Club Road. When it's clear, cross to the left shoulder and drop onto a grassy singletrack that runs west along the ditch below the road.

2.3 Turn left into the parking lot for Spring Meadow Lake State Park (swimming, fishing, non-motorized boating, picnicking). This is a fee area; pay at the entrance booth at the west end of the parking lot. Bikes are not allowed on the walking path that circles the lake. From Spring Meadow, either retrace your tracks or complete a loop by continuing west to LeGrande Cannon Boulevard (see Ride 5).

Early Summer Wall Hillclimbs

Location: On Helena's west end, above LeGrande Cannon Boulevard.

Distance: 100- to 400-yard hillclimbs.

Time: 10 minutes to 2 hours. How long can you play?

Tread: All on dirt doubletrack.

Aerobic level: Strenuous.

Technical difficulty: -3 to 4; some ruts, rocks, loose dirt. Moon Shot's steepness is itself a technical difficulty.

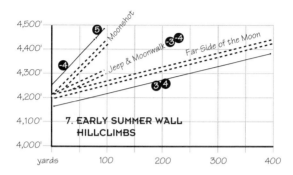

Hazards: Control your speed on descents. Please don't skid, and stay off the slopes when muddy. Be prepared for emergency bailouts on Moon Shot, going up or down.

Highlights: This area dries out earlier than most off-road rides around Helena, and the hillclimbs are varied and challenging. Come April, it's a great place to remind your thighs and lungs what they did last summer. Moon Shot is an ego bruiser, one of Helena's best test pieces for steeps.

Land status: Private. During summer 1996 some trails and jeep roads in this area were posted against trespass. Future access is uncertain.

Maps: USGS Helena.

Access: From the top (west) end of Holter Street, pedal west on LeGrande Cannon Boulevard (see Ride 5). Watch for potholes and traffic on this gravel road. Go 1.4 miles west to a locked gate across the road. Ride around the gate and stay on the inside of the roadway to avoid pedestrians. Continue another 0.2 mile west on LeGrande (across a small concrete bridge) to the first obvious jeep track cutting uphill on the left. This is Jeep. The other hillclimbs also begin here and are described from right to left looking at the hill.

The rides:

Jeep: The first Early Summer Wall hillclimb off LeGrande and often the first to dry out—sometimes rideable through winter. It's strenuous but short, with a tech rating of 3.

Length: 100 yards.

Drop into your granny gear and crawl uphill. Find a pace you can maintain to the top—you'll need extra bursts to power through two dips about two-thirds of the way up. Most folks gravitate to the left side of the track, then cross to the right as the grade eases on top. Here it joins the Early Summer–Seven Sister Ridge Trail (Ride 8). Or continue straight to drop into the West Bowl.

Moon Walk: The easiest route to the ridge from here. Also a good descent option after climbing Jeep. On the moderate end of strenuous, and a -3.

Length: 120 yards.

From the base of Jeep, go left and pedal south on the fairly level but rutted doubletrack. After about 100 yards turn right and climb a grassy doubletrack toward the ridge. Go about 70 feet; Moon Shot is directly ahead. For Moon Walk, bank right and climb the sidesloped doubletrack that cuts north across the ridge face. It tops out at the junction with Jeep.

Moon Shot: Time this ride right and you can aim for the moon as it lowers behind the ridge some spring evening. Steep doesn't begin to describe this climb—your tires will try to grow toenails just to hang on. Strenuous? More like aneurysm-bursting. The tech rating is 5+ just for balance, never mind the obstacles.

Length: 100 yards.

• Early Summer Wall Hillclimbs
• Early Summer–
Seven Sisters Ridge

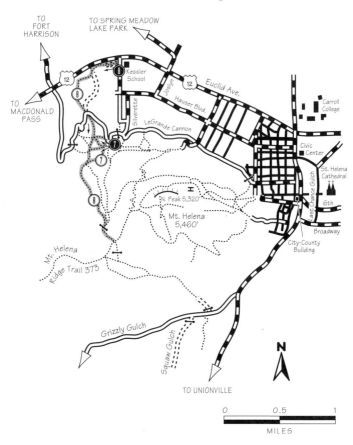

Follow the directions for Moon Walk ("10, 9, 8 . . . "), but put a fire under your tires and launch up the vertical doubletrack straight ahead. Most folks favor the left side, then crash and burn about halfway up. If you're still climbing after your booster engines have flamed out, swing right and try to dodge the asteroids near the top. For the safest re-entry from the ridgetop, turn right on the Early Summer–Seven Sisters Ridge Trail and zip down Moon Walk.

Far Side of the Moon: The longest of these hillclimbs, Far Side starts out gradually, then goes for broke. It's strenuous; give it a 4 due to ruts, low rock steps, and loose gravel.

Length: 400 yards.

From the base of Jeep, pedal south on fairly level but rutted doubletrack. Go straight where Moon Walk and Moon Shot branch right. The initial climb is just a warm-up. Most tire tracks follow the right-hand track to avoid a large erosion gully on the left. The track bends right and climbs harder; favor the center or left tracks on this leg. You've got lots of options for inching around or over the frequent rock steps. Near the top the track jogs right, then left, dropping easily into a crossroads (at mile 1.2) on the Early Summer–Seven Sisters Ridge Trail (Ride 8).

Early Summer–Seven Sisters Ridge

[See map page 50]

Location: On Helena's west end, beginning near Kessler School on U.S. Highway 12 and climbing to Mount Helena.

Distance: 2 miles.

Time: 35 to 50 minutes up, 15 to 25 minutes down.

Tread: 1 mile on doubletrack; 1 mile on singletrack.

Aerobic level: Strenuous with a few short moderate sections.

Technical difficulty: 3 to -5; loose and fixed rocks, root steps.

Hazards: Pinch flats from sharp rocks in tread; watch for other cyclists and hikers, especially when crossing LeGrande Cannon Boulevard and on upper sections of trail.

Highlights: Outstanding early season singletrack. It's a good workout and technical challenge with views of Mount Helena's cliffs from below. There are lots of side trails and access to the

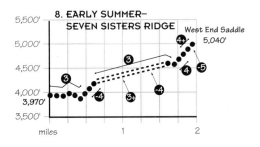

Mount Helena Ridge National Recreation Trail (see Rides 11 and 12) plus a chance to see deer.

Land status: Private and Mount Helena City Park. From mile 0 to 1.8 this route traverses private property. During summer 1996 some trails and jeep roads in this area were posted against trespass. To date, cyclists and hikers have continued to use the trails above (south of) LeGrande Cannon Boulevard, as described below, to reach the West End Trail in Mount Helena City Park. Future access is uncertain.

Maps: USGS Helena.

Access: From Benton Avenue one block north of the Civic Center, pedal 1.6 miles west on Hauser Boulevard to the west end of town. Turn right on Granite Avenue and zoom downhill toward U.S. Highway 12 and Kessler School. Just before the stop sign on US 12, turn left onto a rocky, rutted doubletrack that leads into a bowl-shaped motocross playground. The real riding starts here.

The ride:

0.0 From Granite Avenue pedal west on the doubletrack into the motocross bowl. Several washed-out hillclimbs run 70 to 100 feet up the south slope of the bowl—good hills for practice on the steeps. Head out for Early Summer–Seven Sisters Ridge by staying low, paralleling U.S. Highway 12 on the doubletrack.

0.1 Follow the singletrack straight (west) out of the bowl.

0.2 The track splits into two singletracks. Veer right on the narrower, overgrown track. (The left track climbs to meet a wide singletrack going east-west, which eventually rejoins the route described here.) Climb briefly above US 12 to a pair of rock-strewn doubletracks dropping right (west). Take either one downhill, trying not to gape at the rocket-launch hillclimb ahead. Drop into granny gear and jam it up this 50-foot steep (!!) pitch. I swear it can be done clean if you control your fear of falling over backward.

0.3   Did you make it? Now lean right and descend again to a doubletrack in the gully bottom.

0.4   Stay straight on the singletrack and begin a strenuous climb onto a bluff over US 12. The trail bends south as it gains ground, easing to a moderate grade with views south to Mount Helena.

0.6   Grunt up a 0.1-mile steep climb, dodging loose rocks and imaginary prickly pear cacti.

0.7   The grade eases onto a hogback. Pick your way through the pointy rocks and around a gnarled tree, ignoring two different doubletracks coming up on the left.

0.8   Climb several low rock steps for the last pitch up to LeGrande Cannon Boulevard (see Ride 5). The trail lands smack in the middle of a sharp bend in the road, so watch for cyclists and runners from both directions. Cross the road and take the singletrack breaking uphill slightly to the right. This trail stays on the ridge, climbing somewhat strenuously through the trees.

0.9   Trail turns to doubletracks going right and left. Take either one.

1.0   Doubletracks rejoin at a crossroads on top of Jeep (see Ride 7). To stay on Early Summer–Seven Sisters Ridge go straight on the rocky track that climbs south. A doubletrack splits right here, a more gentle beginning to the upcoming climb. Either way, pedal hard up the steep section until . . .

1.1   The grade eases. Moon Shot (see Ride 7) comes up on

your left; a trail from the West Bowl joins in on your right. Stay straight on the main doubletrack.

1.2 Another backcountry crossroads. Far Side of the Moon (see Ride 7) comes in from the left, a doubletrack drops away on the same side at 11 o'clock, and Dozer Direct (a.k.a. the Directissima) goes right (dropping like a stone in 300 yards to join LeGrande near the west-end gate). Bear slightly right (about 1 o'clock) and climb on a doubletrack that stays near the ridgetop.

1.4 Lunge up a steep 50-foot shot and angle left as the grade eases. Enjoy a brief downhill run.

1.6 Track climbs to an open spot. A doubletrack plummets left and downhill, but you should go straight on the swoopy singletrack into the trees and downhill for about 0.1 mile.

1.7 Begin a strenuous climb, dodging encroaching tree branches and grenade-sized pine cones in the tread. This section rates a 4 thanks to trenched trail and low root steps.

1.8 Fenceline and hiker's gate at the Mount Helena City Park boundary. The trail on the left drops to the Gully (see Ride 3), a wild downhill that makes a fine loop out of this ride if you're tired of climbing.

To reach the Mount Helena Ridge Trail, walk your bike through the gate, remount, and get ready to test your skills and lungs against the rock-strewn climb ahead. The trail runs straight uphill, contours left, then cuts sharply uphill again before settling into a strenuous, rooted, rocky, narrow track (a -5) that will make your heart hammer long before the top comes in sight.

2.0 Top of the climb; junction with the Mount Helena Ridge National Recreation Trail (Rides 11 and 12) and the top of Dump Gulch (Ride 10). To reach the summit of Mount Helena from here, pedal 0.2 mile east (left) on the West End Trail (a strenuous, 4+ climb) to the Y junction with the Prairie Trail (Ride 2). Continue straight on the West End Trail about 150 yards up a hard climb to the 1906 Trail and go right (see Ride 1). This route makes the longest approach by trail to the summit of Mount Helena, a total distance of about 2.7 miles one way.

Grizzly Gulch–Unionville Loop

Location: In the hills immediately south of Helena.

Distance: 11.4-mile loop.

Time: 50 minutes to 1.5 hours.

Tread: 6 miles on gravel road; 5.4 miles on paved road.

Aerobic level: Mostly easy, with some moderate to near-strenuous climbing up Grizzly Gulch.

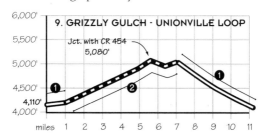

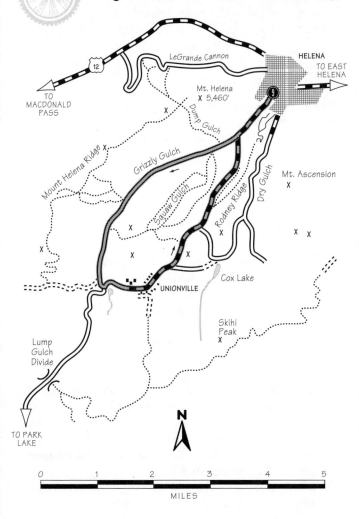

Grizzly Gulch–Unionville Loop

HELENA

TO EAST HELENA

12

TO MACDONALD PASS

LeGrande Cannon

Mt. Helena
X 5,460'

Dump Gulch

Mount Helena Ridge

Grizzly Gulch

Squaw Gulch

Rodney Ridge

Dry Gulch

Mt. Ascension
X

Cox Lake

UNIONVILLE

Lump Gulch Divide

Skihi Peak
X

TO PARK LAKE

N

0   1   2   3   4   5

MILES

57

Technical difficulty: 1 on paved roads; 2 on gravel roads.

Hazards: Watch for traffic, especially in town and where sight distance is limited by curves in the road. Expect loose gravel and washboards on gravel roads; dust can be heavy after cars pass.

Highlights: A non-technical road ride through the South Hills, with a fast, paved downhill run to close the loop.

Land status: County roads through private and Helena National Forest lands.

Maps: Helena National Forest; USGS Helena.

Access: Ride from town, beginning at the City-County Building on Park Avenue.

The ride:

0.0   From the City-County Building on Park Avenue pedal south on Park. Stop at Broadway, but continue south on Park, climbing as it leaves downtown. The road narrows as it threads the gap at the head of Last Chance Gulch.

1.0   The road forks. The paved road (left) goes to Unionville. You'll come back that way, but for now lean right onto gravel Grizzly Gulch Road and continue south past old charcoal kilns. The gulch was named back in the 1860s for a large bear that regularly feasted on chokecherries along the bottom of this dry drainage. Stay on Grizzly Gulch Road as it winds south for the next 4 miles. (See Rides 11, 12, and 13 for information on side trails in this stretch.)

4.3   The road skirts a large gold dredging hole on the right. Begin climbing a more moderate grade.

4.7 The Excelsior Lode and pond (private home) on left.

4.9 Grade eases briefly between driveways on either side, then resumes a steep climb south.

5.2 Grade eases. A row of mailboxes marks a sandy road on the right that leads to the Mount Helena Ridge Trail and Ride 11. Stay straight on the main road through an open area scattered with homes (site of the long-ago mining camp Park City). The road soon bends left and climbs through forest at a moderate clip.

5.7 Junction with Unionville Road (County Road 454). The right-hand road climbs hard to the Lump Gulch Divide (see Rides 25 and 26). Instead, turn left and buzz downhill. The grade levels off and the road meanders north.

6.3 Swing east and climb moderately.

6.8 The climb tops out.

7.0 Drop onto pavement and wipe the dust from your eyes. Hang on for 4.4 miles of smooth downhill sailing. Bank left into the hamlet of Unionville. Watch for cars and lazy dogs.

7.8 Springhill Road goes right (see Appendix A).

8.6 Dry Gulch Estates road goes right (see Ride 18). CAUTION: watch for traffic turning off Unionville Road here.

9.0 Waterline Trail (Ride 17) on right.

10.4 Grizzly Gulch goes left. Stay on pavement going north and swoop into town.

11.4 City-County Building; end of loop.

Dump Gulch

Location: 1 mile south of Helena on the backside of Mount Helena City Park.

Distance: 1.2 miles.

Time: 15 to 30 minutes going up; 10 minutes coming down.

Tread: 1.2 miles on single and doubletrack.

Aerobic level: Mostly strenuous.

Technical difficulty: 3, but the final climb rates a 4 due to loose rocks and sidehill tread.

Hazards: Yield to other trail users. Use care when guiding your bike through the hiker's pass gate at the Mount Helena City Park boundary. If exiting from Dump Gulch onto Grizzly Gulch Road, look both ways for traffic before entering the roadway.

Highlights: This is the most gradual approach to Mount Helena's upper flanks, and one of the most lightly used. Riders coming off the Mount Helena Ridge National Recreation Trail

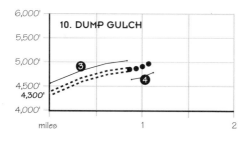

• Dump Gulch

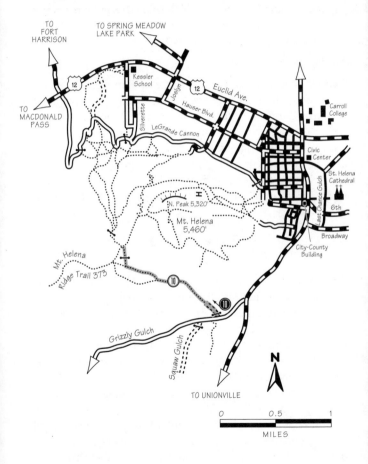

TO
FORT
HARRISON

TO SPRING MEADOW
LAKE PARK

12

TO
MACDONALD
PASS

Kessler
School

Joslyn

12 Euclid Ave.

Hauser Blvd.

Silverette

LeGrande Cannon

Carroll
College

Civic
Center

St. Helena
Cathedral

6th

Last Chance Gulch

N. Peak 5,320'

Mt. Helena
5,460'

Broadway

Mt. Helena
Ridge Trail 375

10

10

City-County
Building

Grizzly Gulch

Squaw Gulch

TO UNIONVILLE

N

0   0.5   1
MILES

373 (Ride 11) can descend Dump Gulch to avoid trail traffic common on other Mount Helena routes. The grassy bowl at the head of Dump Gulch is a good place to see deer.

Land status: Private and Mount Helena City Park. The metal gate at the mouth of Dump Gulch (mile 0) sometimes wears orange paint or a no trespassing sign. Ask permission before entering private property.

Maps: USGS Helena.

Access: Most folks ride to the trailhead from town. From the City-County Building on Park Avenue, pedal south on Park 1 mile to a Y junction. The Orofino Gulch or Unionville Road (paved) goes left. Instead, turn right onto Grizzly Gulch Road (gravel) and pedal about 0.3 mile south. The road passes old charcoal kilns on the right, then climbs through a broad right turn. Near the top of the turn watch for a gate and doubletrack leading west into Dump Gulch on the right.

The ride:

0.0 Walk your bike under the steel crossbar on the gate across the mouth of Dump Gulch. Begin pedaling up a moderate grade on debris-studded singletrack that veers toward the left-hand side of the gulch.

0.1 The climb steepens to an almost strenuous pitch. Deer are sometimes seen between rock outcrops on the slopes above and to the right.

0.4 The trail skirts a huge pile of white tailings, then grinds up a hard left turn. The climb is steep but lasts only 50 feet. On top the trail widens into a well-defined doubletrack and enters a shady grove of pines.

0.6 Doubletrack goes left; bear right past a sign that reads,

"Area Closed to Motor Vehicle Use." Rocks dot the tread for a short stretch before the doubletrack turns grassy as it winds among the trees on a more moderate ascent.

0.9 As the trail enters a bowl-shaped meadow at the head of Dump Gulch it reverts to singletrack. Watch for deer, especially at sunrise and sunset.

1.0 A singletrack splits left and bolts uphill (steep!!) to join the Mount Helena Ridge National Recreation Trail 373. Instead, bear right. Begin a strenuous climb back into the trees toward the ridge.

1.1 Pedal hard to reach the fence marking the boundary of Mount Helena City Park. Dismount to steer your bike through the pass gate (it's easiest if you stand the bike on its rear wheel and weave the handlebars between the posts as needed). Remount and scramble up the rocky, loose hillclimb ahead.

1.2 The trail tops out in a grassy saddle where it meets the Mount Helena Ridge National Recreation Trail 373 (Rides 11 and 12). A left here leads to Park City, 6 miles distant. Turn right to continue climbing to Mount Helena and the Prairie and 1906 trails (Rides 2 and 1). Or, for a quick downhill back to town, go straight (north) and drop onto the Early Summer–Seven Sisters Ridge Trail (Ride 8).

Mount Helena Ridge National Recreation Trail 373

Location: South of Mount Helena along the ridgeline immediately west of Grizzly Gulch Road.

Distance: 13.9-mile loop.

Time: 1.5 to 3 hours.

Tread: 1.3 miles on paved road; 5.1 miles on gravel road; 7.5 miles on singletrack.

Aerobic level: Moderate with a few strenuous climbs.

Technical difficulty: 1 to 2 on roads; 3 to -5 on singletrack.

Hazards: Watch for traffic on roads. Control your speed on singletrack descents; be prepared to slow for sudden rocky sections.

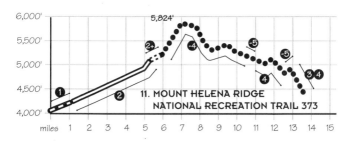

Highlights: A ride on Helena's wild side, surprisingly close to town. The ridge trail is 7.5 miles of outrageous singletrack, with great views of surrounding mountains and valleys, including a distant Helena townscape. You've got a good chance of seeing deer, coyote, and other wildlife here; wildflowers are abundant in spring.

Land status: Helena National Forest; Mount Helena City Park; private.

Maps: Helena National Forest; USGS Helena.

Access: Most folks ride this loop clockwise, starting and ending in town. This way most of the climbing occurs on good gravel roads and the descent is all singletrack. To avoid much of the climb, drive to mile 5.8 following the route described below and park your car at the trailhead in Park City. A few endorphin-fueled riders prefer to do this ride counterclockwise, starting by climbing through Mount Helena City Park on the 1906, Prairie, or Early Summer–Seven Sisters Ridge trails.

The ride:

0.0   From the City-County Building on Park Avenue pedal south on Park. Stop at Broadway (0.1 mile), but continue south on Park, climbing as it leaves downtown. The road narrows as it threads the gap at the head of Last Chance Gulch, a stone's throw from new condos and old row homes on either side.

1.0   The road forks. The paved road goes left to Unionville. Instead, lean right onto gravel Grizzly Gulch Road and continue south, climbing past old charcoal kilns.

1.3   Dump Gulch gate and track off to the right (see Ride 10). The Black Forest singletrack goes left (Ride 16). In another 50 yards the Squaw Gulch Access Trail goes left

Mount Helena Ridge National Recreation Trail 373

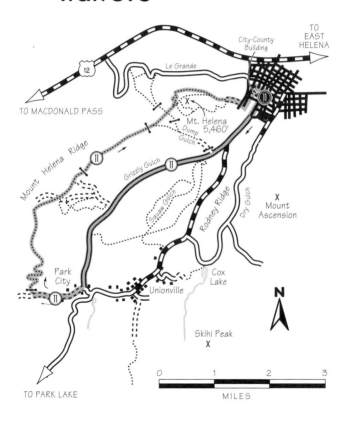

TO EAST HELENA

City-County Building

Le Grande

12

TO MACDONALD PASS

Mount Helena Ridge

Mt. Helena 5,460'

Dump Gulch

Grizzly Gulch

Squaw Gulch

Rodney Ridge

Dry Gulch

X Mount Ascension

Park City

Unionville

Cox Lake

N

Skihi Peak X

TO PARK LAKE

0   1   2   3
MILES

(Ride 13). Continue climbing steadily on Grizzly Gulch.

3.3 Forest Service access road on right; this is a shortcut escape route from the Mount Helena Ridge Trail (see mile 9.3 below and Ride 12).

3.7 Sand dam access road on right (another possible exit from the ridge at mile 8.5).

4.0 Jeep track goes right; metal guardrail on left (and Glory Hole Mine behind it). This marks the access to Squaw Gulch (Ride 13).

4.1 Old jeep road goes right up a narrow gulch. Stay on main road.

4.3 Large gold dredging hole on the right. Begin climbing a more moderate grade.

4.7 The Excelsior Lode and pond (private home) on left.

4.9 The grade eases briefly between driveways on either side, then resumes a steep climb south.

5.2 Grade eases. A row of mailboxes marks a sandy road on the right. Turn right here and pedal west. Ignore the many private drives on both sides of the road.

5.5 Driveways go right and left; stay on the main road, which narrows to one lane and climbs moderately.

5.7 A driveway with a sign for house number 2050 goes right. Follow the road as it bends left. In 70 yards turn right at the "Trail" sign onto the trailhead access road and pedal uphill.

5.8 Trailhead parking lot and wood rail fence. Go through the gate (on the left) and continue uphill on the good doubletrack, which skirts the southwest edge of a large meadow.

6.0 Doubletrack goes straight; a lone ponderosa pine marks a right turn onto a singletrack that cuts east across the base of a vast, grassy slope. This is Mount Helena Ridge National Recreation Trail 373. It switchbacks broadly up the open, south-facing hillside ahead—a broiler by 10 a.m. on hot July days. The grade is on the lung-stretching end of moderate, with a few strenuous pitches.

6.4   Gun it up a tight, on-the-fall-line switchback going right. Loose gravel makes it interesting.

6.6   The trail drops onto the east face of the ridge and contours north, climbing more steeply as it goes. Follow the final switchback left and keep the rear wheel rolling for the last push up a steep slope.

7.0   Top of the hill. A small tree provides welcome shade and a good spot to enjoy the views. Look southwest for a glimpse of Red Mountain, south to Skihi Peak, and east to the head of Squaw Gulch and Mount Ascension Ridge. Once you're rested and ready, pedal west on narrow singletrack atop this grassy, level bench.

7.3   Turn right at a wooden post (the left-hand track goes 50 yards to a better vantage point of the same view as at mile 7). The trail aims north, rolling gently, between huge ponderosa pines. Enjoy the relatively smooth tread while it lasts.

7.6   The trail contours into the open on the ridge's east flank, offering a fine view of Helena in the distance. Begin a fast, rollicking downhill.

7.7   Grab the brakes and swallow that grin. Slow down for a steep, rocky drop rated at a 4+ if you're not afraid of endos.

7.8   Zigzag through two S turns into a short patch of rocks, then bank left into trenched tread across a small clearing. Drop into the trees, lean into a right turn, and hang onto the left edge of the track to avoid a rough bed of limestone.

8.0   The trail twists downhill around trees, then swings left onto a welcome smooth descent.

8.1 The grade levels out, climbs on loose scree, then levels again.

8.2 Begin a strenuous climb on the ridgetop over loose gravel and fist-sized chunks of limestone.

8.3 Veer right off the ridgetop onto mostly smooth tread that gently contours down the east flank of the ridge.

8.5 The trail goes over a low bump, then drops to a confusing junction with an old jeep track. (A left here leads west to a breezy vantage point on a small spur ridge; the jeep track turns to an erosion scar.) Bank right instead, but then stay straight where the jeep track dives to the right again, dropping into the trees (see Ride 12). Follow the main trail north on a bumpy, twisting, rolling contour high on the east flank of the ridge.

9.0 Break into a ridgetop meadow and zip across this low saddle.

9.1 Choose your path as the trail re-enters the trees and turns to doubletrack. The preferred line wanders from one track to the other. Begin a steep, rocky drop (a solid 4; watch for the slanted bedrock ledge just when things seem to ease up).

9.3 As the trail rockets downhill into a bowl-shaped, grassy clearing, a doubletrack drops away on the right. Most folks are going too fast to notice, but this side trail offers a quick (1-mile) descent to Grizzly Gulch Road (see Ride 12). To stay on the ridge, continue straight.

9.4 The trail climbs the north side of the bowl, then cuts right and scampers up and down through the trees.

9.5 Ride up to a fenceline and stile. Carry your bike up and over the stairs and enjoy views east to Casey Peak in the Elkhorns and north to the Helena Valley. Pedal north onto a broad, open slope. Watch for wheel-grabbing rocks at odd intervals.

9.7 Swing left and downhill in trenched tread, then cut through a peninsula of trees.

9.9 Bank hard for a sweeping right-hand turn (watch for cow pies in summer). Gear up for a straight run east on mostly smooth tread.

10.2 Drop over to the west flank of the ridge and into shady forest on twisty, sometimes sidesloped trail.

10.3 Break back into the open atop the ridge, rolling over an exposed hogback and down a rutted trail. (Ride on the main tread here, staying out of a new parallel track on the right.)

10.5 The original trail runs straight into a fence. Skirt left on the recently built bypass, which curves around a corner of private property.

10.6 Begin making your way through a rock-strewn obstacle course. Slow down and waltz among the rust-colored chunks of granite littering the tread. Most of the rocks are rooted in place, but a few like to move around the dance floor—it never rides the same way twice. But the grade is fairly level; at its worst, rate it a -5.

10.8 The rocks thin out and the trail climbs gradually.

10.9 Top out on a rounded knob with outstanding views northeast to the cliffs of Mount Helena, with Lake Helena in the distance. You can look east to the Elkhorns and west to MacDonald Pass and the Continental Divide. To the north, Head Lane runs arrow-straight into the Scratchgravel Hills, and the Sleeping Giant snoozes on the horizon. Look for wildflowers beside the trail: shooting star, arrowleaf balsamroot, and bitterroot are abundant here. Pedal north, banking into an off-camber right turn and dodging rocks on a gradual descent.

11.3 Carry your bike over another stile. Look straight ahead for a back-of-beyond view of Mount Helena's summit. Remount and ride about 100 yards to a left turn at a sign post pointing back toward Park City. A trail goes right, over a rocky knob and down the ridge into Dump

Gulch. A doubletrack dives straight ahead and into the head of Dump Gulch (see Ride 10). But you go left on the main trail.

11.4 Bounce through another session of Dances With Rocks, this one shorter and easier at -4.

11.5 Pedal into an open, grassy saddle. Look carefully to see the Dump Gulch Trail (Ride 10) coming in on the right and the Early Summer–Seven Sisters Ridge Trail (Ride 8) on the left; tall grass may obscure both. Either makes a fine re-entry to town. For the classic ending, however, grind those gears and climb straight ahead toward Mount Helena. The trail gets rockier as it goes, with a root-rock ledge combo, then a nasty pitch of broken bedrock (both -5).

11.8 The climb eases at a picnic table where the trail meets the Prairie Trail (on the left), the most popular exit route from here. It's nearly all downhill now, only 1.5 miles to the Mount Helena parking lot at the end of Adams Street (see Ride 2).

13.3 Parking lot. To close the loop and return to the City-County Building, coast down the dirt road 0.2 mile (go left around the gate that blocks the road), cross Howie but stay straight on Adams, then turn left on Benton. Ride two long blocks north to Clarke.

13.9 The City-County Building is across the corner.

Mount Helena Mini Ridge

Location: 3 miles southwest of Helena on the ridge west of Grizzly Gulch.

Distance: 10.5-mile loop.

Time: 1 to 2 hours.

Tread: 1.3 miles on paved road; 2.3 miles on gravel road; 0.2 mile on doubletrack; 6.7 miles on singletrack.

Aerobic level: Mostly moderate, with some strenuous climbs between miles 3.3 and 5.1.

Technical difficulty: 1 and 2 on roads; 3 to -4 on the singletrack climb. Much of the tread between miles 3.3 and 4.3 is narrow and sidesloped, making it easy to roll off the edge. Mount Helena Ridge Trail 373 rates mostly 3, with short sections of -4 to -5 (see Ride 11).

Hazards: Watch for traffic on roads. Don't fall into the mine

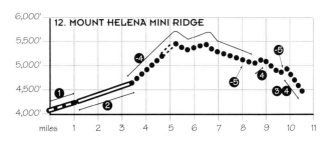

hole at mile 3.9—it's especially easy to do if you ride this loop in reverse and bomb down the singletrack here. Portions of Mount Helena Ridge are open and exposed; don't ride here if lightning threatens. Yield to other trail users.

Highlights: If you're wondering why any dyed-in-the-wool mountain biker would shorten a classic route like the Mount Helena Ridge Trail (Ride 11), here's the answer. This link between Grizzly Gulch and the ridge is one of the sweetest singletracks in the area, uphill or down. It also offers a shady alternative to the sun-baked switchbacks at the official trailhead above Park City. This trail sees limited use; side trails offer opportunities for exploring.

Land status: Helena National Forest and City of Helena.

Maps: Helena National Forest; USGS Helena.

Access: Begin this ride in town at the City-County Building on Park Avenue.

The ride:

0.0 From the City-County Building on Park Avenue pedal south on Park, which becomes the Orofino Gulch–Unionville Road as it leaves town.
1.0 Bank right, off the pavement, onto gravel Grizzly Gulch Road. Pedal south on the mostly easy grade.
3.3 Pass a single-story home on the left and swing into a gradual right turn. As the turn straightens out look for a doubletrack going right and uphill to a fence. Turn right here and pedal 50 feet to a travel restriction sign and hiker's pass gate in the fence. Walk your bike through, remount, and pedal about 30 feet up the doubletrack, which continues into a wooded gulch (of-

73

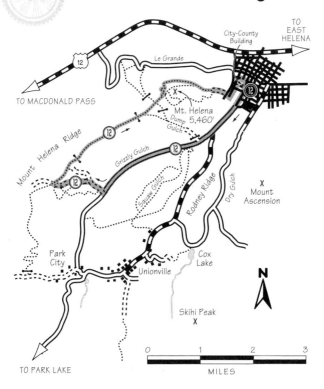

• Mount Helena Mini Ridge

TO EAST HELENA

TO MACDONALD PASS

City-County Building

Le Grande

X

Mt. Helena 5,460'

Dump Gulch

Mount Helena Ridge

Grizzly Gulch

Squaw Gulch

Rodney Ridge

Dry Gulch

X Mount Ascension

Park City

Unionville

Cox Lake

N

Skihi Peak X

0   1   2   3

MILES

TO PARK LAKE

fering a more moderate—and less interesting—climb to the ridge). Turn left on the first trail, a faint track in the grass. Drop into your granny gear and grunt hard into the trees on the now-obvious singletrack. The trail swings right and begins a strenuous but rideable contour along the ridge flanking the south side of the gulch.

3.6   Jam it up a steep 25-foot pitch.

3.7   Climb through a sharp switchback left. It's rideable, but sharp enough to warrant a -5 rating. The trail contours east at an easier grade through dense fir and pine forest.

3.8   Follow the trail as it wraps to the right around the nose of the ridge and breaks into ponderosa parkland. Lean into an open right turn and head back toward the gulch.

3.9   Turn left on the edge of a deep mine hole and climb hard up the ridge. This rates a 4+ for loose tread and steepness.

4.0   The trail dips right, rolls over an odd hump in the trail, and cruises back into the gulch on thin, sidesloped tread.

4.1   Gear down for another strenuous climb through open forest.

4.3   The grade eases onto a broad bench above the gulch, and in another 0.1 mile runs nearly level, wandering through the trees.

4.6   Spin up a brief climb and along a wide, tree-lined corridor.

4.7   Trail junction. The right-hand track drops down, eventually joining the doubletrack on the bottom of the gulch. Turn left instead and continue the moderate climb.

4.8   Another trail junction. Bounce onto an old dirtbike trail in the middle of a banked turn. Turning left leads up a hogback ridge high above the sand dams along Grizzly Gulch Road. Instead go right and climb hard on gravelly tread to doubletrack on an old roadbed. Turn left and continue on the doubletrack, which snakes right and left, climbing more strenuously toward the top.

5.1   Roll onto the Mount Helena Ridge National Recreation Trail 373. The left-hand path goes 2.7 miles to the Park

City Trailhead (see Ride 11). Head back to town by turning right and following Trail 373 north on a bumpy, twisting, rolling contour high on the east flank of the ridge.

5.6   Break into a ridgetop meadow and zip down and across the low saddle.

5.7   The trail re-enters the trees and turns to doubletrack. Begin a steep, rocky drop (a solid 4; watch for the slanted bedrock ledge just when things seem to ease up).

5.9   As the trail rockets downhill into a bowl-shaped, grassy clearing, a doubletrack drops away on the right; most folks are going too fast to notice. This doubletrack rockets downhill 1 mile to rejoin Grizzly Gulch Road at mile 3.3 above. For the scenic route back to town, stay straight on Trail 373.

6.0   The trail climbs the north side of the bowl, then cuts right and scampers through the trees.

6.1   Ride up to a fenceline and stile. Carry your bike up and over the stairs and enjoy views east to Casey Peak in the Elkhorns and north to Helena. Pedal north onto a broad, open slope, watching for wheel-grabbing rocks at odd intervals.

6.3   Swing left and downhill in trenched tread, then through a peninsula of trees.

6.5   Bank hard for a sweeping right-hand turn. Next, gear up for a straight run east on mostly smooth tread.

6.8   Drop over to the west flank of the ridge and into shady forest on twisty, sometimes sidesloped trail.

6.9   Break back into the open atop the ridge, rolling over exposed hogback and down a rutted trail. (Ride on the main tread here, staying out of a new parallel track on the right.)

7.1   The original trail runs straight into a fence. Skirt left on the recently built bypass around this corner of private property.

7.2 Begin a rock-strewn obstacle course. The grade is fairly level; at its worst, rate it a -5.

7.4 The rocks thin out and the trail climbs gradually.

7.5 Top out on a rounded knob with outstanding views northeast to Mount Helena (Lake Helena in the distance), east to the Elkhorns, and west to MacDonald Pass and the Continental Divide. Pedal north, banking into an off-camber right turn and dodging rocks on a gradual descent.

7.9 Carry your bike over another stile. Remount and ride about 100 yards to a left turn at a signpost pointing back toward Park City. A trail goes right, over a rocky knob and down the ridge into Dump Gulch. Another trail (doubletrack) dives straight ahead and into the head of Dump Gulch (see Ride 10). But your route goes left (the main trail).

8.0 Bounce through another rocky section; this one's a -4.

8.1 Pedal onto a grassy saddle. Look carefully to see the Dump Gulch Trail (Ride 10) coming in on the right and the Early Summer–Seven Sisters Ridge Trail (Ride 8) on the left; tall grass may obscure both. Either makes a fine re-entry to town. For the classic ending, however, grind those gears and climb straight ahead toward Mount Helena. The trail gets rockier as it goes, with a root-rock ledge combo and then a nasty pitch of broken bedrock (both -5).

8.4 The climb eases at a picnic table where the trail meets the Prairie Trail on the left. It's nearly all downhill now, 1.5 miles to the Mount Helena parking lot at the end of Adams Street (see Ride 2).

9.9 Parking lot. To close the loop and return to the City-County Building, coast down the dirt road 0.2 mile, cross Howie but stay straight on Adams, then turn left on Benton. Ride two long blocks north to Clarke.

10.5 The City-County Building is across the corner.

Variation: Make an upper loop by following the directions in Ride 11 to mile 8.5 in that description (the same spot as mile 5.1 in this description). Then rip back down to Grizzly Gulch Road on the route described above to return to town. The disadvantage to this 13.6-mile variation is the amount of time spent on Grizzly Gulch Road, which tends to be dusty and bumpy.

Squaw Gulch Loop

Location: 2 miles south of Helena between Grizzly Gulch and Orofino Gulch roads.

Distance: 7.7-mile loop.

Time: 45 minutes to 1.5 hours.

Tread: 4.4 miles on paved road; 1.6 miles on gravel road; 1.7 miles on singletrack atop old road bed.

Aerobic level: Moderate.

Technical difficulty: Mostly 2+ and 3 with one -5 rock step.

Hazards: Yield to other trail users, and watch for horseback riders. Ride in control on descent.

Highlights: One of the most gradual and least technical climbs into Helena's South Hills, this route offers plenty of shade, access to other trails (including the sweetest slice of singletrack in the neighborhood), and a chance to see deer and

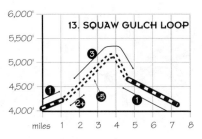

other wildlife. The Meadow at mile 3.5 feels far from town and makes a good destination for evening rides.

Land status: Private, Helena National Forest, and Bureau of Land Management. To date, the owner of the private property near the mouth of Squaw Gulch has generously allowed access for non-motorized recreationists to the national forest lands beyond. Other owners of inholdings and parcels along Grizzly and Orofino gulches have closed trails leading into Squaw Gulch. The trail segment from The Meadow to the Unionville Road (mile 3.6 to 4.3) crosses private land and future access is uncertain. Please heed all marked private property boundaries.

Maps: USGS Helena.

Access: Ride from town. Start at the City-County Building on Park Avenue.

The ride:

0.0 From the City-County Building on Park Avenue pedal south on Park. Stop at Broadway (0.1 mile) but continue straight on Park. Begin moderate climbing.

0.6 The road narrows, lined with old buildings. Watch for traffic.

1.0 Y intersection; the Orofino Gulch or Unionville Road (paved) goes left. Instead turn right onto Grizzly Gulch

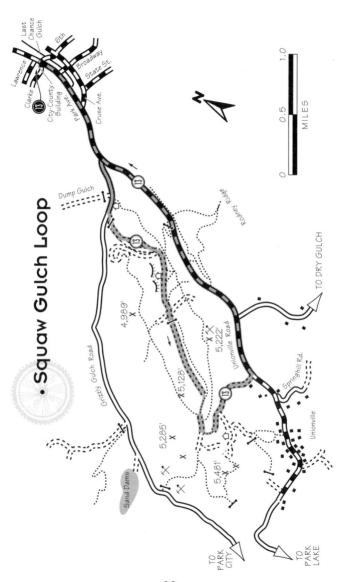

• Squaw Gulch Loop

Lawrence
Last Chance Gulch
6th
Clarke
Broadway
State St.
13
City-County Building
Park Ave.
Cruse Ave.

Dump Gulch
13
13
Rouden Road
4,989' X
5,128'
5,222' XX
Unionville Road
TO DRY GULCH
Grizzly Gulch Road
5,285' X
X
5,481' X
13
Springhill Rd.
Unionville
Sand Dams
TO PARK CITY
TO PARK LAKE

N

0   0.5   1.0
MILES

Road (gravel) and pedal south. The road passes old charcoal kilns on the right, then climbs through a broad right turn.

1.3 Gate and doubletrack for Dump Gulch on right (see Ride 10). Continue straight on Grizzly Gulch Road another 70 yards. Watch for a well-concealed singletrack diving left off the road's shoulder next to a pressure-treated wooden fencepost. It's about 30 feet before a brown metal gate, also on the left. Ease onto the trail, which zigzags through the underbrush onto doubletrack. Turn right on the doubletrack, following the numerous fat tire tracks.

1.4 Turn left onto Squaw Gulch Road (graded in 1997). Begin climbing on an easy grade.

1.7 Follow the main road as it climbs left at an almost moderate pitch.

2.0 The grade levels out and a spur road goes right (the exit for Ride 15). Stay straight.

2.2 A doubletrack climbs left into a sloped meadow, connecting with the Black Forest–Natalie's Nightmare Trail (Ride 16). Stay straight on the main gulch trail.

2.4 Another Black Forest link trail goes left; continue straight.

2.5 A side track goes right (one option for your return trip out), but keep going straight. A trail immediately on the left is yet another Black Forest link.

2.6 The main road bends left. Also, the Squaw Singletrack comes down from behind a fence fragment on the outside of the turn (see Ride 14). Veer right onto doubletrack and ride around the right end of a metal gate. Continue climbing on singletrack that winds along the old road bed.

2.8 Easy rock lip (a 3+ at worst); begin rocky section.

2.9 Here's the crux move . . . a rock step up. It's a -5 but remarkably rideable. Just go straight at it (most folks aim for left of center) and tractor on up. Traction is usually good unless the rock (or your tire) is wet. Think of it as a big curb. Above the step the grade eases somewhat, and the tread stays fairly smooth from here on out.

3.4 One last steep push as the Squaw Singletrack (Ride 14) joins on left. Stay straight on the main doubletrack.

3.5 Welcome to The Meadow. This makes a good turn-around point for riders who want to try the Squaw Singletrack (Ride 14), which is almost too fun to be legal.

Rides 15 and 16 offer alternative routes out of Squaw Gulch, following the ridges on either side. Both leave from this point in The Meadow. To take the standard exit route described below, pedal south on the grassy doubletrack that bisects The Meadow.

3.6 Turn left onto a well-defined singletrack that cuts through the grass and turns into a dirt jeep road at the edge of the forest on The Meadow's east side. Test those brakes and dive down into the trees, following a quasi-singletrack line as it twists down the bottom of this narrow gully. Ride in control and watch for rocky patches and possible downfall on the trail.

3.8 Two doubletracks go right and uphill at about one o'clock and four o'clock. Lean left and stay on the main gully track. It snakes through an even narrower section, then eases slightly as the gully opens up.

4.0 Lean into a sharp right turn, then cruise east on grassy tread.

4.2 Watch for ruts as the trail skirts the backyard of a house above the Unionville Road. The trail stays well left of the yard, but please ride slowly and quietly to avoid disturbing the residents (who have been generous enough to allow bike access here for so long).

4.3 The tracks bend right and join a driveway leading to the house. Turn left onto the driveway, look both ways for traffic, and drop onto the paved Unionville Road. Go left and bomb downhill for the most direct route back to Helena.

6.7 Grizzly Gulch goes left; stay right on pavement into town.

7.7 Pull up to the City-County Building on Park Avenue to complete the loop.

Squaw Gulch Singletrack

Location: 2 miles south of Helena between Grizzly Gulch and Orofino Gulch roads, immediately uphill and east from Squaw Gulch Road (Ride 13).

Distance: 0.8 mile—never long enough. A total of 7 miles when ridden from town and back in combination with the Squaw Gulch Road route.

Time: 10 to 20 minutes going up, lightspeed coming down.

Tread: 0.8 mile on singletrack.

Aerobic level: Easy going down, moderate to strenuous going up.

Technical difficulty: Mostly 3 with a few off-camber turns and rocky spots that rate 3+ to -4.

Hazards: Yield to other trail users and watch for horseback riders. Ride in control on descent—no skidding, please.

Highlights: This is the sweetest singletrack in the neighborhood, a whoop-n'-holler downhill run or a fine climb. The trail runs through open pine forest with a few short sections where small trees encroach on both sides. At times the trail skirts within 20 feet of the ravine that holds Squaw Gulch Road (Ride 13).

Land status: Private and Helena National Forest.

Maps: USGS Helena.

Access: Ride from town using Squaw Gulch Road (Ride 13) for the quickest and easiest access. Since this trail shines as a downhill run, let's start at the upper end from The Meadow on Squaw Gulch (mile 3.5 in Ride 13). Turn around once you reach The Meadow, and ride back down Squaw Gulch Road.

The ride:

0.0 Shift into a higher gear and point your bike downhill (north) on Squaw Gulch Road (Ride 13).

0.1 Bank right onto a singletrack where the road drops left.

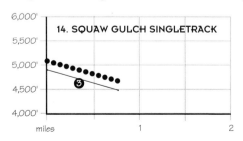

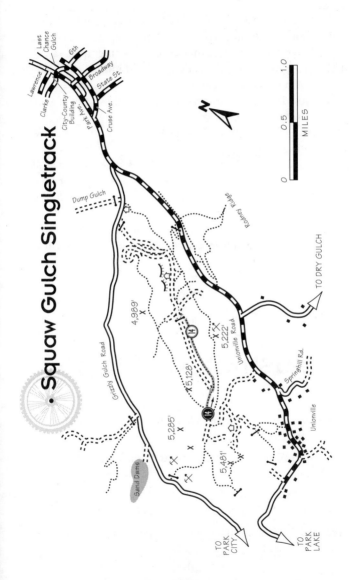

•Squaw Gulch Singletrack

Last Chance Gulch
Lawrence
6th
Broadway
Clarke
State St.
City-County Building
Park Ave.
Cruse Ave.

Dump Gulch

Grizzly Gulch Road

Router Ridge

4,989'
X

5,128'
X

5,222'
X X
X

Unionville Road

Springhill Rd.

5,285'
X

X

5,481'
X

Sand Dams

Unionville

TO DRY GULCH

TO PARK CITY

TO PARK LAKE

N

0   0.5   1.0

MILES

Watch your speed—the trail dodges a couple of trees right at the start—then let it fly. Keep an eye out for hikers, horses, and other cyclists coming up.

0.2 Spare the soil (and a bedraggled old juniper) and slow down *before* the bush.

0.5 Slow for an off-camber right turn followed by a short bumpy section.

0.7 An early bailout track drops left to Squaw Gulch; most folks stay straight.

0.8 Just when you're beginning to hope that this downhill run will go on forever, the trail drops to the fence and finish line. Hold on for the hummocky runout to join Squaw Gulch Road. Turn around and watch your riding cohorts show off the goofiest grins this side of happy hour at the Windbag Saloon. Now ride up Squaw Gulch and do it again.

15

Bushwhack Ridge

Location: 2 miles south of Helena on the ridge between Squaw Gulch and Grizzly Gulch Road.

Distance: About 2.2 miles, depending on your route-finding skills. Figure on a total of about 7 miles round trip pedaling from town, up Squaw Gulch, and back.

Time: 15 to 45 minutes for this 2.2-mile segment.

Tread: 1.5 miles on singletrack; 0.2 mile through the tall grass; 0.5 on dirt road.

Aerobic level: Moderate with a strenuous climb to start it off.

Technical difficulty: 3+ on trail; up to 4+ off trail; 2+ on road.

Hazards: The tread alternates abruptly between smooth and bumpy, requiring attentive braking on downhills. The 0.2-mile bushwhack demands good route-finding skills or a willingness to find your way out after getting lost.

Highlights: See the wilder side of Squaw Gulch! Views from the ridge include Mount Helena, parts of the West Ridge National Recreation Trail, and Mount Ascension. Also watch for deer and other wildlife.

Land status: Helena National Forest and private. Future access across private land on this ridge is uncertain. Please heed all posted property boundaries.

Maps: USGS Helena.

Access: Ride from town; Squaw Gulch Road (Ride 13) provides the quickest and easiest access. This trail is best ridden from top to bottom; start at The Meadow on Squaw Gulch.

The ride:

0.0 From The Meadow, pedal north on the right-hand track of an old jeep road that climbs a rocky slope on the west flank of Squaw Gulch.

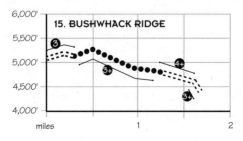

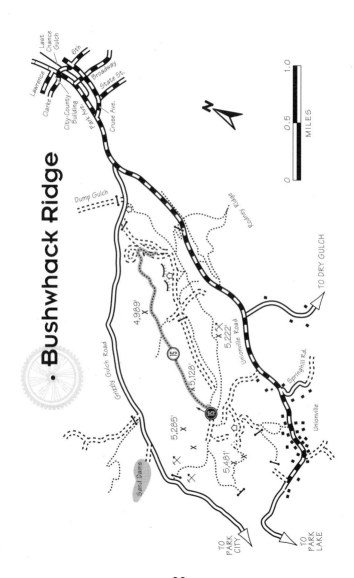

Bushwhack Ridge

Last Chance Gulch
6th
Lawrence
Broadway
Clarke
State St.
City-County Building
Park Ave.
Cruse Ave.

Dump Gulch

Rovers Ridge

TO DRY GULCH

Grizzly Gulch Road

4,989'
X

15

X 5,128'

15

5,222'
X X

Unionville Road

Springhill Rd.

5,285'
X

X

Sand Dams

X X

5,481'
X X

Unionville

TO PARK CITY

TO PARK LAKE

MILES
0   0.5   1.0

88

0.2 The grade eases in a ridgetop meadow. From here the trail rolls northeast along the top of the ridge, rambling over and around knuckles of limestone.

0.3 Enjoy a brief downhill and more rolling, sometimes rocky tread.

0.5 Pedal up to the high point on the ridge, glimpsing distant horizons through the trees.

0.6 Begin a steep, rocky descent. Veer right where the grade levels for a few yards. (The left track stays higher on the ridge, runs through a mini boulder field, then rejoins the main trail in about 70 yards.) The main trail drops through a sidesloped pitch, then contours back into the trees.

0.7 Lean left at the next fork; the straight-on path is recovering from erosion. The main trail snakes downhill on a carpet of pine needles.

0.8 A well-defined singletrack goes sharply left only to dead-end at "no trespassing" signs. So stay right and zip into the open again. Gallop down two low limestone steps and continue north as the trail from mile 0.7 above comes in on the right.

0.9 The main trail appears to swing right and downhill toward Squaw Gulch below. Instead, keep to the left and search for a faint trail ducking into the trees. Sometimes this is marked with colored tape or flagging. Once in the trees, the trail becomes more evident, though it braids in places and is trenched in others.

1.2 Again the main trail seems to continue right and downhill. And again we fade left instead, following deer tracks into tall grass. (If you're not comfortable bushwhacking, turn around here and climb back to Squaw Meadow.) Do not be misled by several tracks that plummet off the ridge on the west side. Instead, aim for town and an area in the foreground with fewer trees.

Pedal north to the edge of a large blow-down of burned, dead trees filling a bowl. Hold to the high ground and skirt around the blow-down going left. Game trails offer the best paths through open forest just uphill from the blow-down. Eventually these lead to a more open ridge. Lean right here and weave downhill and northeast around a couple of fallen trees.

1.6   Toward the bottom, stay on high ground and look for an obvious road on the right side of the ridge. Drop onto this bumpy dirt road, which swings left and snakes through a big loop turn in the trees. Some of this land is private—please heed any no trespassing signs. Stay on this road as it contours steadily downhill to rejoin the main Squaw Gulch Road

2.2   Turn left onto the main Squaw Gulch Road and bounce 0.6 mile down to Grizzly Gulch Road for the final leg back to town.

Black Forest Ridge– Natalie's Nightmare

Location: 2 miles south of Helena on the east ridge above Squaw Gulch.

Distance: 2.4 miles one way. From town and back, this ride is part of a 7.2-mile loop.

Time: 20 to 50 minutes for this 2.4-mile segment.

Tread: 2.4 miles on doubletrack and singletrack.

Aerobic level: Strenuous climbs and rocky (energetic) downhills.

Technical difficulty: Mostly -4, but 4+ to 5 on climbs, and up to 5+ on descents.

Hazards: Loose, rocky, and steep (!!) sections, including one recklessly steep section at mile 0.9 that is best walked. Also watch for downfall, especially through the old burn at mile 1.9.

Highlights: This ride offers fun downhill runs along a wooded ridge, challenging climbs, views of surrounding mountains, solitude, access to other trails, and a good chance of seeing deer. For strong riders, Black Forest Ridge–Natalie's Nightmare is a good alternate route in and out of Squaw Gulch.

Land status: Helena National Forest and private property. Future access across private land on this ridge above Squaw Gulch is uncertain. Please heed all posted property boundaries.

Maps: USGS Helena.

Access: If this is your first time on Black Forest Ridge–Natalie's Nightmare, ride it from the top down as an exit route from Squaw Gulch (Ride 13). From where the Squaw Gulch Road enters The Meadow (at mile 3.5), continue 0.1 mile south on doubletrack. Watch for fading doubletrack breaking left that grows more obvious as it enters the trees on the east edge of The Meadow.

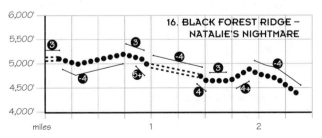

The ride:

0.0 Pedal northeast on fading doubletrack as it climbs into the trees on the east side of The Meadow. The track rolls along the ridge, then drops on a grassy, sweat-drying 0.2-mile descent.

0.3 Begin a strenuous climb along the ridge. The tread grows progressively rockier and steeper (a solid 4 in the dust of midsummer due to poor traction).

0.6 Climb onto the first knob; the grade eases.

0.7 Second knob (and high point on the ridge). Enjoy views east to Skihi Peak and Rodney and Ascension ridges. Look south between your feet for a glimpse of the Unionville Road far below, then northeast to the distant glimmer of Lake Helena and the Big Belt Mountains. Point your bike north and dodge left on the trail as it skirts a fenced-in mineshaft.

0.8 The trail fakes left onto a small saddle; a cairn here marks a nearly invisible singletrack breaking west and down into the trees. This game trail bashes through underbrush, eventually dropping onto the Squaw Gulch Singletrack (Ride 14). Veer right (north) instead to stay on the ridge.

0.9 Roll onto a bump of slate-gray bedrock and steer right as the ridge abruptly falls away. Welcome to Natalie's Nightmare. Most folks start out trying to ride this drop, then attempt a dismount on the really nasty (steep!! and bouldery) pitch below. A few riders with underactive adrenal glands actually ride the whole 5+ drop, but not those of us with a healthy, normal fear of disfiguring injury. The "trail" dives down the fall line, then swings left and plunges into the trees.

1.0 Grade eases; grassy tread.

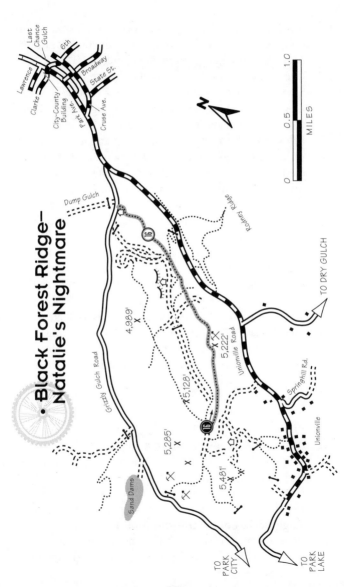

Black Forest Ridge—
Natalie's Nightmare

Last Chance Gulch
6th
Lawrence
Broadway
Clarke
State St.
City-County Building
Park Ave.
Cruse Ave.

Dump Gulch

Grizzly Gulch Road

4,989'

Rooney Road

Unionville Road

5,222'

5,128'

5,285'

5,481'

Sand Dams

Springhill Rd.

Unionville

TO DRY GULCH

TO PARK CITY

TO PARK LAKE

N

MILES
0   0.5   1.0

1.1 Hang on for another big descent (a 4+). This one's not quite as steep or rocky as the first, but sling your butt over the rear wheel to prevent an endo.

1.2 The trail runs out of the trees onto easier doubletrack. Slow down for two short, rocky drops (both 4).

1.3 Crawl down the steep berm of new logging road, go straight across, and pause at a crossroads of sorts. Just below the road a singletrack cuts left and into the trees for a swoopy, gentle downhill to Squaw Gulch Road (Ride 13). Going right, it crosses private property as it drops like a rock to the Unionville Road. Please heed the landowner's wishes and stay off this steep (!), eroded run. Instead, continue straight (north) on the well-defined Black Forest doubletrack.

1.4 Grab the brakes for one last rocky drop (4) into a ridgetop meadow.

1.5 Another singletrack crossroads. Going left leads to the Squaw Gulch Road going uphill (Ride 13). Straight ahead drops you down to the Squaw Gulch Road and a quick escape to Grizzly Gulch Road. If your lungs can handle one more hard climb, bank right on singletrack that stays close to the ridgetop heading north. The grade stays level at first.

1.6 Another singletrack goes right and drops onto private property along the Unionville Road. Stay straight on the ridge.

1.7 Begin a strenuous climb up a steep, extremely loose scree slope. The first 0.1 mile is the worst, with low rock steps, no traction, and heart-hammering steeps. Nearer the top both grade and tread improve.

1.9 Just before the final summit veer left onto a faint singletrack. Follow this trail to the west flank of the ridge, entering a forest of burnt snags (hence the moniker "Black Forest"). A cairn sometimes marks the way, and the trail becomes more obvious as it slides down the west side of the ridge. Downed trees are common across the trail.

2.0 The trail swings left through the old burn, dodging downfall and root wads. If you lose the track, aim for the low saddle to the northwest; look for a small rock outcrop and the edge of unburned forest.

2.1 Bank right and downhill onto well-defined singletrack. The trail takes a steep, smooth line into a shaded gully, snaking around small boulders but always offering an easy route.

2.4 The gully drops straight ahead, but lean right instead onto an old roadbed above a ruin (a charcoal kiln from gold-rush days). This doubletrack switchbacks hard left to the base of the kiln, then heads right to drop into a gully. Gear down for the quick uphill out of the gully onto Grizzly Gulch Road. Turn right to coast 1.3 miles back to downtown Helena.

Waterline Trail Loop

Location: In the South Hills south of Helena, along Unionville Road, on the west flank of Rodney Ridge.

Distance: 5.4 miles on a figure-eight loop.

Time: 30 minutes to 1 hour.

Tread: 3 miles on paved road; 0.1 mile on doubletrack; 2.3 miles on singletrack.

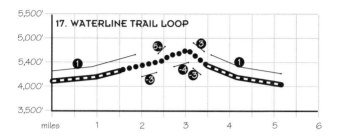

Aerobic level: Mostly moderate, with three short but strenuous climbs.

Technical difficulty: 1 on paved roads; a 4+ switchback on the access trail; -3 on the Waterline Trail; 3 to -4 on other singletrack sections.

Hazards: Watch for traffic on roads. Please yield to horse riders on all trails. Stop, dismount, and move well off trail to let them pass. Some sections of trail are narrow, with steep dropoffs on one side. Expect other trail users, especially when rounding blind corners. Ride in control.

Highlights: Until 1995 the Waterline Trail was one of Helena's most popular hiking and biking trails. Its nearly level grade and shady route above the Unionville Road enticed many beginning riders and families to try singletrack for the first time. Sadly, private landowners along the north end of the trail decided to fence their property lines and prohibit trespassing, abruptly cutting off access to the trail from town. This short loop takes advantage of an access trail built in 1997 on land managed by the Prickly Pear Land Trust. Enjoy the spicy singletrack, which is perfect for beginners at slower speeds and a blast for more advanced riders at race pace. Watch for deer and other wildlife as you ride.

Land status: Helena National Forest; Prickly Pear Land Trust; private. More trail construction on Prickly Pear Land Trust property may open new access trails in the near future. Check with the land trust or local bike shops for current information (see Appendix B for addresses and phone numbers).

Maps: Helena National Forest; USGS Helena.

Access: Ride this figure-eight loop starting from the City-County Building on Park Avenue in Helena.

The ride:

0.0   Pedal south on Park Avenue, which becomes Unionville or Orofino Gulch Road as it leaves town.
1.0   Grizzly Gulch Road (gravel) goes right; stay left on the paved Unionville Road and begin a moderate climb south.
1.3   Look for a grassy pullout on the left side of the road marked by signs for Helena city limits (the signs face south). If you pass the wooden sign for the Helena National Forest boundary you've gone too far. The pull-out is the parking area and trailhead for a small parcel of land owned by the Prickly Pear Land Trust. Dive onto singletrack that swoops into an abrupt gully (the dry bed of Last Chance Creek) and U-turns south along the bottom of the hillside. This trail was built by volunteers in 1997 to provide public access to the downhill end of the Waterline Trail. Gear down for the climb ahead—on the gentler side of strenuous.
1.4   The trail threads through low brush and wild rose bushes, then climbs a steep, earthen ramp above the road. The grade eases onto grassy tread and then drops through a dry runoff dip. Swing to the outside of the trail to crank through the sharp 90-degree left turn ahead.

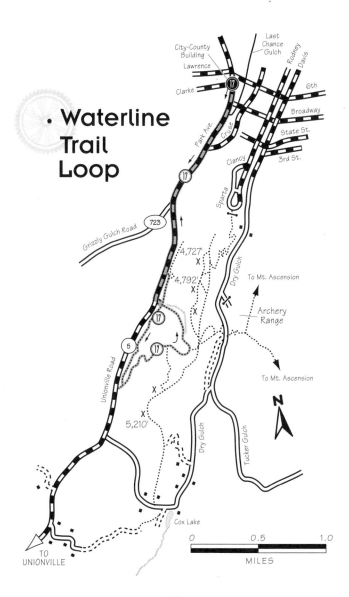

1.5 Enjoy a short level grade that leads to a stone bridge across a narrow gully. Stomp on your pedals as you leave the bridge to hoof it up a steep 30-foot pitch as the deeply cut trail swings north across an open hillside. Regain a more moderate pace as the trail continues to climbs through a series of three switchbacks. The first is a broad and fairly easy turn to the right. The second switchback hairpins on itself to the left—narrower tread makes this a 4+ turn the first time you ride it, but once you know what to expect the turn is ridable. The third switchback curves right and onto an easier grade.

1.6 Roll onto the Waterline Trail and spin south on level, mostly smooth singletrack.

1.8 A spur trail dives off to the right back down to the Unionville Road; stay straight.

2.0 The Waterline loops left into a big gully. As it swings back out watch for a trail coming down from the left and crossing to continue downhill to the right. This will be our exit path on the last leg of our loop. For now, continue straight on easy, level tread as the trail curves out of the gully and onto a long, fairly straight shot south in the trees above the Unionville Road.

2.3 The trail wanders in and out of several more side gullies, with intervals of straight track, some through dense pine and fir forest, some across more open slopes. When looping through the tight gully turns, keep an eye ahead for other trail users.

2.5 After swinging out of another gully, the trail shoots south again. A side trail drops easily down to the Unionville Road—an optional way back to town.

2.6 The trail bends right and tiptoes along the brink of a cliff-like road cut. There's not much room to spare here, so walk your bike if this balance-beam exercise rattles your nerves.

After crossing the road cut, the trail curves inland again and forks. The right fork soon bushwhacks above another road cut that has eroded into the trail. So go left instead and push your bike up the steep (!) but short hill on the obvious dirt track through the trees. Remount on top and pedal hard uphill to. . .

2.7   A junction with a well-defined singletrack (also described in Ride 19). Go right to drop quickly (it's loose and rocky) onto Unionville Road for the fastest way back to town. Or, to complete the singletrack loop, turn left and climb on loose, rocky tread going northeast. Ignore the steep rocky trail going uphill on the right. The main trail crosses an open slope on an easier grade, then banks into the trees.

3.0   Hang on for a quick dip and a banked turn left, then climb up a short rocky stretch.

3.1   After a short stretch of moderate grade, gear down for a steep, strenuous climb on trenched, rocky trail. This section gets looser as summer wears on, but it's always rideable . . . if your legs and lungs are up to it.

3.2   Scramble over a limestone step or two and onto Rodney Ridge. Drop east on smooth singletrack through spindly lodgepole. In some places the forest is encroaching on the trail, so be ready to duck branches or swerve around clumps of small trees.

3.3   Bomb downhill through two sudden dips and brake for a left turn at the edge of Rodney Meadow (see also rides 19 and 20). Look for a grassy, user-created path that curves left (north) just as the main trail reaches the edge of the woods (and goes straight, rutted, into the meadow). The grassy path arcs 30 yards and joins a slightly trenched trail coming in from Rodney Meadow. Turn left and into the woods. The trail is smooth and sinuous at first, winding above a small ravine on the right. Rocks and loose gravel become more abundant as the trail plunges downhill—ride in control, and watch for other trail users, especially horses.

3.6 Bounce down the last steep section and onto the Waterline Trail. Veer to the left and in 20 feet bank right onto the access trail you came up on. Zip down to the doubletrack road to reach. . .

3.7 The Unionville Road. Turn right onto pavement and coast downhill back to town.

5.4 Roll up to the City-County Building to end the ride.

Dry Gulch Road Loop

Location: South of Helena between Rodney Ridge and Mount Ascension.

Distance: 6.9-mile loop.

Time: 40 minutes to 1 hour.

Tread: 3.5 miles on paved road; 2.9 miles on gravel road; 0.5 mile on doubletrack.

Aerobic level: Moderate overall, with a fairly strenuous 1-mile climb.

Technical difficulty: 1 on paved roads; 2 on gravel roads and doubletrack.

Hazards: Watch for traffic, particularly where the road narrows at mile 1.1. The road also skirts an archery range and an informal rifle range. Do not ride onto the archery range, and avoid riding when the rifle range is being used; bullets have rico-cheted near hikers and cyclists. Also be alert for loose dogs, especially near town and in the neighborhood around Cox Lake.

Highlights: A good, non-technical lunch-hour ride into Helena's South Hills, with access to several trails (see Rides 17, 19, 20, and 23). Or do it near dawn or dusk and watch for deer.

Land status: County road. Roadside property is a mix of private, city, and Helena National Forest.

Maps: USGS Helena.

Access: This loop begins and ends at the corner of Park Avenue and Broadway, 0.1 mile south of the City-County Building on Park.

The ride:

0.0   From Last Chance Gulch ride five blocks east (uphill) on Broadway to the stop sign at Rodney Street. Continue straight (east) on Broadway, coasting down one block.

0.4   Turn right on Davis Street. Pedal south about three blocks on Davis to a stop sign at State Street. Continue south on Davis, which becomes gravel and is known as Dry Gulch Road as it leaves town.

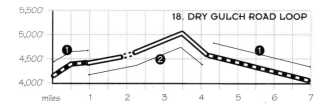

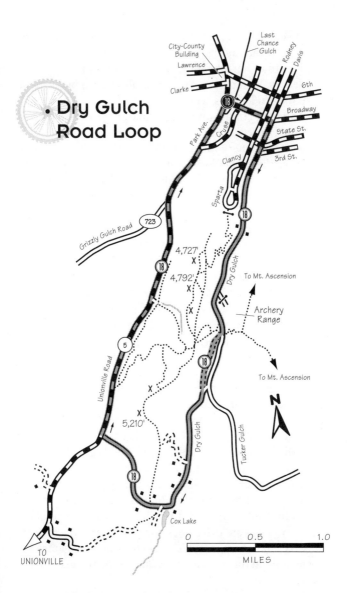

Dry Gulch
Road Loop

City-County Building

Last Chance Gulch

Lawrence

Clarke

Rodney

Davis

6th

Broadway

State St.

3rd St.

Park Ave.

Cruse

Clancy

Sparta

723

Grizzly Gulch Road

4,727'
X

4,792'
X

X

Dry Gulch

To Mt. Ascension

Archery
Range

To Mt. Ascension

Unionville Road

5

X

X

5,210'
X

Dry Gulch

Tucker Gulch

N

Cox Lake

0   0.5   1.0

MILES

TO
UNIONVILLE

103

0.8 Pavement ends; pedal south on gravel Dry Gulch Road as it threads along the bottom of the gulch.

1.1 The road narrows briefly between two private residences. Watch for traffic, especially at the blind turns at either end of this section.

1.3 The road climbs up to signs marking the Helena National Forest boundary. The grade eases slightly.

1.6 Pass an archery range on the left. CAUTION: Do not enter the range, even if it appears empty. The area is private property, open only to members of Lewis and Clark Archers. Members may be target shooting even if no cars are in the parking lot.

1.8 Doubletrack climbs away from the road on the right (see Ride 19). Stay left on Dry Gulch Road.

1.9 An access road drops to an old gravel quarry on the right, with doubletracks climbing the slope beyond (see Rides 19 and 20). Gun enthusiasts frequently use these flats for target shooting—play it safe and avoid the area when people are shooting. If it's clear, drop off Dry Gulch Road and pedal south on the doubletrack leading up the dry creek bottom. Or stay on the main road—the two routes rejoin in 0.5 mile. The doubletrack winds up the creek bottom among cottonwoods and pines at an easy pace.

2.4 Gear down for an abrupt climb up the road berm at the junction of Dry Gulch and Tucker Gulch roads. Turn right to stay on Dry Gulch Road, and begin climbing a more strenuous pitch.

3.1 The grade eases but continues climbing south through a neighborhood of mobile homes and cabins.

3.4 As the climb tops out, turn right to stay on the main road (a private drive goes straight here). Welcome to Cox Lake, host to some boisterous hockey games by moonlight during winter. Pedal west on the main road, past the turnoff for the Cox Lake Cutoff–Springhill Road (see Appendix A).

3.5   The road plunges down the west side in a steep right-hand curve back into the shade of trees on both sides. Be alert for traffic, heavy gravel, and washboards.

3.9   Lean hard into a sharp left turn, then continue snaking downhill.

4.2   Turn right onto paved Unionville Road and coast downhill.

4.6   Singletrack goes right (see Rides 17 and 19). Stay on road.

4.9   Another singletrack goes right to join the Waterline Trail (see Ride 17). Stay on road.

5.3   Doubletrack goes right to join Waterline Trail (see Ride 17). Stay on road.

5.6   National forest boundary sign.

6.0   Back at the edge of town. Grizzly Gulch Road goes left; stay right and follow the pavement north.

6.6   Cruse Avenue goes right; it's a good shortcut back to Davis Street and the central part of town.

6.9   Close the loop at Park and Broadway.

Dry Gulch Short Loop

Location: South of Helena between Rodney Ridge and Mount Ascension.

Distance: 4.6-mile open loop.

Time: 20 to 50 minutes.

Tread: 0.9 mile on singletrack; 0.3 mile on doubletrack; 0.9 mile on gravel road; 2.5 miles on paved road.

Aerobic level: Moderate, with one 0.2-mile strenuous climb.

Technical difficulty: Mostly 3. A few rocky patches on the descent rate a -4.

Hazards: Watch for traffic, particularly where the road narrows at mile 0.5 and when dropping onto Unionville Road. At mile 1 the route skirts an archery range, then climbs above an informal rifle range. Avoid riding here when either range is being used; bullets have ricocheted near hikers and cyclists. Ride in control on rocky descents.

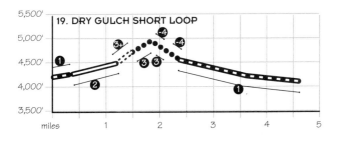

Highlights: A short loop over Rodney Ridge with access to other trails (see Rides 17, 18, and 20). It makes a good lunch-hour ramble with some sweet singletrack and a quick, paved return leg. There's a fair chance of seeing deer and other wildlife.

Land status: Private, City of Helena, and Helena National Forest. Please heed all posted private property boundaries.

Maps: USGS Helena.

Access: From Last Chance Gulch ride five blocks east (uphill) on Broadway. At the stop sign at Rodney, continue straight on Broadway. Coast down one block and turn right onto Davis Street. Pedal south about three blocks on Davis to State Street. Odometer readings begin here.

The ride:

0.0 Pedal south on Davis Street, climbing easily.
0.3 Pavement ends; Davis is known as Dry Gulch Road once it leaves town.
0.5 Watch for traffic on blind curves where the road narrows between houses. From here the road climbs moderately.
1.0 Archery range entrance on left; stay on Dry Gulch Road.
1.2 Veer right and uphill on rough doubletrack. If you miss this route, turn right into the old gravel quarry just up the road and take one of the obvious jeep hillclimbs that scar the slopes on the right (west). The city owns this property but has occasionally threatened to prohibit public access; watch for "no trespassing" signs. The aforementioned doubletrack begins as a less strenuous climb.

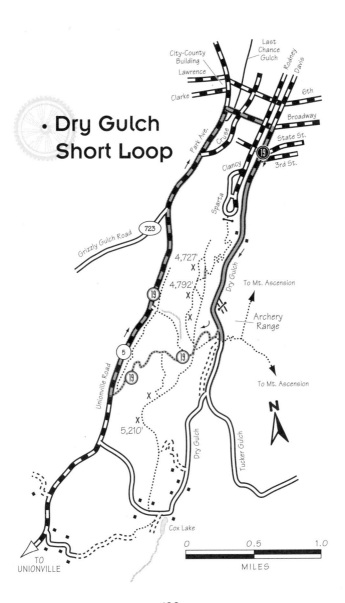

Dry Gulch
Short Loop

City-County
Building
Lawrence

Clarke

Last
Chance
Gulch

Rodney

Davis

6th

Broadway

State St.

19

3rd St.

Park Ave.

Cruse

Clancy

Sparta

Grizzly Gulch Road

723

4,727'
X

4,792'
X

X

Dry Gulch

To Mt. Ascension

Archery
Range

19

5

19

19

X

X
5,210'

Unionville Road

To Mt. Ascension

N

Dry Gulch

Tucker Gulch

Cox Lake

TO
UNIONVILLE

0   0.5   1.0

MILES

108

1.3 Jeep hillclimbs join from left. Bank right and uphill. A series of jeep tracks fan out and up the ridge. The most gradual of these is the cream-colored track that wraps to the right. It's still a strenuous grunt; most riders favor the left-hand side of this doubletrack to avoid a deep erosion gully on the right.

1.4 The grade eases into Rodney Meadows. A fading doubletrack goes right to join Ride 20; stay straight (south) on the main track.

1.5 Doubletrack goes sharply right and beelines northwest to the ridgeline option for Ride 20. Instead, pedal south another 25 feet and turn right on well-defined singletrack. This trail cuts across the heart of the meadow and is trenched into the tall grass in places. Bear left where the trail first forks (doubletrack goes right then into the trees and down to the Waterline Trail—see Ride 17).

1.6 The trail forks again near the edge of Rodney Meadow; this time bear right. The trail begins climbing through a forest of spindly pines at a moderately strenuous angle.

1.8 Crest over the Rodney Ridge divide (at a modest low spot) and bounce down loose, rocky tread on the west side.

1.9 The grade levels off and runs fast and smooth.

2.0 Brake for a rocky stretch, then dip into a wooded gully and a hard right turn. The trail threads through shady woods, then jogs south across an open slope.

2.2 Slow for more loose rocks; ignore the steep trail that drops in from the left.

2.3 A trail splits off to the right; this is the head of the Waterline Trail (see Ride 17 for an optional route back toward town). For the fastest return leg, continue straight

on the main trail, rattling down a rock-strewn pitch
to . . .

2.4 Bottom out on Unionville Road. The re-entry to pavement is abrupt; look both ways for oncoming traffic.
Turn right and crank it into your big chainring for a
smooth downhill run.

3.7 Grizzly Gulch Road goes left; lean right to fly into town.

4.2 Cruse Avenue goes right. If you need closure, pedal up
Cruse to State Street, turn right, and follow State five
blocks east to Davis where you began the ride. But if
you're headed for downtown, stay straight on what is
now Park Avenue.

4.6 Corner of Park and Broadway. Time for post-ride liba-
tions.

Rodney Ridge

Location: On the ridge directly south of Helena between
Orofino Gulch (Unionville Road) and Dry Gulch.

Distance: 2 miles one way (4 miles up and back).

Time: 30 minutes to 1 hour going up; 20 to 45 minutes coming down.

Tread: 1 mile on singletrack; 1 mile on doubletrack.

Aerobic level: Strenuous climbs, some moderate grades, and
a few short downhills.

Technical difficulty: Mostly 4 punctuated by sections of -5 to 5+. The first 0.7 mile features at least four unrideable switchbacks and steep exposure. The upper portion climbs hard on loose, rocky tread—a solid 5 in several places.

Hazards: Yield to all other trail users. On the switchbacks, use care to avoid dislodging rocks onto the trail below. Ride in control—the first 0.5 mile runs across extremely steep slopes where a fall or riding off the outside of the trail could result in serious injury or death.

Highlights: A good technical test, mixed with quad-crushing climbs. There's access to other trails (see Rides 17 and 19), great views from atop the ridge, and a good chance of seeing deer and other wildlife.

Land status: Helena National Forest, Bureau of Land Management, private. Please heed all posted private property and fencelines.

Maps: USGS Helena.

Access: From Last Chance Gulch pedal 5 blocks east (uphill) on Broadway. Turn right onto Rodney Street, pedal about 0.4 mile south, and turn right onto gravel Clancy Street. Climb west one block on Clancy, then south three blocks on Sparta Street as it climbs high above the Rodney Street neighborhood. Sparta then wraps left to meet Rodney Street at the edge of town. The trail begins here, from a small parking lot on the south side of the street about 150 yards east of a large Bonanza-style log gate over a private drive.

The ride:

0.0 Slide into your granny gear and then walk your bike through the pass gate on the east end of the large gravel

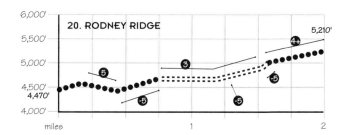

parking area. Be careful not to snag those new shorts on the barbed wire. Remount and pedal southeast on a stiff contour to the east flank of Rodney Ridge. The trail narrows once or twice, with a sheer dropoff on the left-hand side. Don't take any chances.

0.1 The trail begins descending to avoid a parcel of fenced private property.

0.2 Dismount and walk around the first switchback going left and down. Coast down to a second unrideable switchback, then continue downhill trending south on a steep grass and sagebrush slope.

0.4 Begin climbing into the second set of switchbacks. The first two are unnavigable—too tight and poorly graded. Future improvements may include widening these turns to accommodate bikers (don't hold your breath). The legs between each turn are well laid out, making the climb only mildly strenuous. The upper switchbacks aren't as tight or steep; advanced riders will pivot through them without much trouble.

0.6 Head into the trees for a strenuous climb and one last switchback. Then contour gently up to a junction.

0.7 Turn left onto old doubletrack (the right-hand path joins a ridgetop doubletrack and meets private fenceline). Pedal south, favoring the left-hand track to avoid a rocky patch.

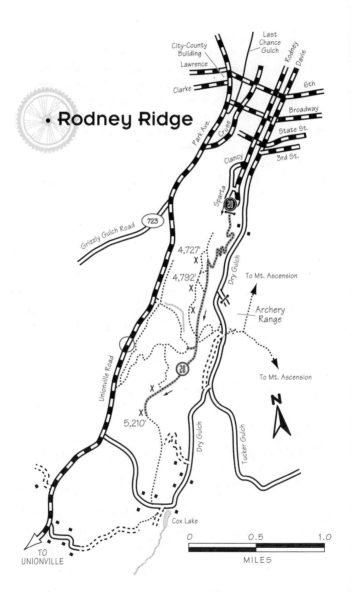

Rodney Ridge

0.8 The old jeep track visible on the right here follows the top of Rodney Ridge as it roller-coasters over hogbacks and down sandy steeps. Follow it south (if you don't mind the extra climbing) to rejoin the main route at mile 1.2 below. Stay on the main doubletrack to avoid any serious climbing for a while.

1.0 Singletrack (from the ridge route) comes in on right; stay straight on doubletrack.

1.2 A grassy doubletrack goes left to a jeep track and the old quarry on Dry Gulch Road (see Rides 18 and 19); stay straight. The trail breaks into Rodney Meadows. Watch for doubletrack on the right leading to the ridge route described at mile 0.8 above. Pedal south into the broad meadow.

1.3 Mid-meadow crossroads. A doubletrack from the ridge comes in from the right and behind. Two singletracks also go right here: a fading trail leads west then north into the trees and down a ravine to join the Waterline Trail (Ride 17) in 0.3 mile; the second trail (a trench) goes going west-southwest into the trees. It bends right and climbs over the ridge, dropping to the head of the Waterline Trail and the Unionville Road.

A left at the crossroads leads to the jeep track on the meadow's eastern edge, with several options for dropping into the gravel quarry along Dry Gulch Road. (People sometimes use the quarry as a target range for sighting-in rifles. Do not approach the quarry if you hear shots.)

To stay on the Rodney Ridge ride, go straight at the crossroads on grassy doubletrack. It sidehills up to the jeep track that runs along the east edge of the meadow. Join this and keep climbing south. Gear down and grunt up two short but steep (!) pitches full of loose rocks. Both climbs rate a solid 5 for technical difficulty.

1.6 Take a breather on a brief level spot, then resume climbing as the track winds into the trees. It starts out strenuous and gets worse near the top. Ruts, roots, and a few loose rocks add to the difficulty of keeping both wheels on the ground during the -5, lung-rupturing climb. Are we having fun yet?

1.7 Gasp onto flat ground. It looks like a road goes left, but we're heading right onto rocky singletrack that just keeps climbing, albeit at a lesser tilt, to the southwest. (Another singletrack, well camouflaged, bushwhacks into the trees going directly west, then north, to meet the trail that links Rodney Meadows with the Waterline Trail.)

To stay on the ridge going south, climb on the loose, rocky trail, over a 4+ limestone ledge, and contour along the east side of the ridge. The tread here is extremely loose—sand and fist- to foot-sized rocks make traction treacherous; it's rated at -5. After about 70 yards the grade eases and the rocks turn to a more rideable gravel.

1.8 Scamper up another hogback knob and enjoy the broad views.

2.0 Doubletrack drops away on the left. Stay straight and climb onto the ridge's highest point, with good views of Mount Ascension Ridge, Upper Squaw Gulch, and Skihi Peak. The dirt road far below threads through Dry Gulch Estates, and the paved Unionville Road is on the right, about 600 feet straight down. This high point is as good a place as any to turn around for the ride back to town.

A rocky singletrack continues south along the ridgetop, but this runs onto private property in 0.4

mile. New owners plan to build a house smack on top of the trail at the base of a steep descent; the access road goes left (east) and drops to Dry Gulch Road. As of this writing, local riders are working with landowners to reroute this end of the trail to preserve access to Dry Gulch Road near Cox Lake. In the meantime, please do not cross private property unless you've obtained permission beforehand.

Mount Ascension Lower Loop

Location: In the South Hills, about 0.5 mile south of Broadway between Last Chance Gulch and the Capitol complex.

Distance: 2.3-mile open loop.

Time: 20 to 40 minutes.

Tread: 1.9 miles on doubletrack; 0.4 mile on singletrack.

Aerobic level: Mostly moderate with a few strenuous climbs.

Technical difficulty: 3 with one or two sections of 4.

Hazards: Yield to other trail users; control your speed on descents.

Highlights: Good trail riding right above one of Helena's oldest neighborhoods, including three short stretches of first-class singletrack and views of town and the North Hills; there's a good chance of seeing deer and other wildlife.

Land status: Beattie Street City Park and private property. Much of the open space adjoining the old neighborhood is slated for a housing development. Landowners higher upslope have posted many trails against trespass. Obey all posted property lines; ask for permission before crossing private land.

Maps: USGS Helena.

Access: From Last Chance Gulch pedal east on Broadway about five blocks uphill to Rodney Street. Turn right on Rodney, pedal one long block south, and turn left onto State Street. Coast down to Davis, then climb again on State and continue three blocks east to Beattie. Turn right on Beattie and go uphill five blocks to where the road dead-ends by an open field. The trail begins at the hiker's gate in the fence at road's end, which marks the boundary of Beattie Street Park.

The ride:

0.0   Ride through the gate and climb hard on singletrack. The trail eases and contours into a small ravine at the treeline.

0.1   Drop into the gully and climb hard again. The trail bends left and levels off. Two less obvious singletracks go right here; stay straight.

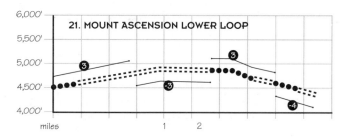

0.2 Hop the kelly hump onto an old roadbed. Several trails branch right and uphill; pedal east on the road.

0.3 A doubletrack cuts across the roadbed (a challenging climb going right; it rejoins the route described here in 150 yards). The easiest route goes straight to meet a rough jeep track. Turn right and climb between ruts, going south toward Mount Ascension.

0.5 The road forks and doubletrack joins from the left and downhill. Go right for a shortcut to mile 1.8 below. For a longer ride, lean left and continue the moderate climb. Ignore the next doubletrack in 50 feet, also on the right.

0.6 A gate straight ahead is posted against trespass. Follow the hairpin turn right onto a level grade and a boulder barricade. The landowner adjusts these periodically to exclude motor vehicles; during the summer of 1997 the boulders were painted orange to prohibit trespassing. If you obtain permission to enter, look for an opening on the right. Resume climbing on the doubletrack, now headed west.

0.8 Gated private road on the left; stay straight and continue climbing. In about 150 feet a singletrack drops off the bank above the road on the left, crosses the road, and plunges downhill into trees on the right. Stay on the main road.

0.9 The grade eases onto a broad bench with sweeping views north and west. Doubletracks fan out east and south. The trails straight ahead and to the right offer shortcuts to the homeward leg. On your right at 1 o'clock a trail bounces down a rocky hogback to mile 1.8 below; at 2 o'clock an old road cut has been filled with debris to discourage travel. The tread straight ahead drops to join the trail at mile 1.7 below. Instead,

• Mount Ascension Lower Loop

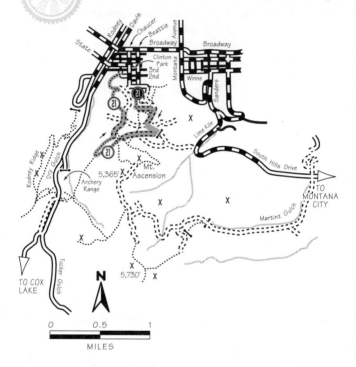

climb up and slightly left onto doubletrack that drops gently into the trees. (Taking a sharp left here will make you climb hard on loose scree to the C on Mount Ascension.) Left of this track, a faint singletrack peels east into the trees, bound for Mount Ascension's summit (see Rides 22 and 23).

1.0 A doubletrack crosses your path. Go straight and zip through the dip. From here the doubletrack picks up momentum and wraps south around the base of Mount Ascension, reverting to singletrack along the way. Watch for deer.

1.4 V junction with singletrack. Make a sharp-angled right to complete the loop going north. (The left-hand track contours south above the Lewis and Clark Archers target range, following barbed-wire fence down to a ravine and a sometimes overgrown link to the Entertainment Trail, Ride 22.) Northbound, the trail snakes among young pines at an easy clip.

1.6 The trail braids twice—veer right both times to avoid tunnel-like riding through dense pines. The trail climbs briefly, then dips and banks right, with the left-hand tracks from above re-entering here.

1.7 Bank hard left and head up an abrupt rise. Then the doubletrack from mile 1 joins from the right, followed soon after by a singletrack on the right that goes back to the broad bench at mile 0.9. Stay straight on the main doubletrack here.

Next you must choose between the big gully straight ahead (fun, but hang on) or the 50-foot singletrack detour that breaks right to skirt the gully. The doubletrack splits again on the other side, only to rejoin on a low spot in a hogback ridge as the odometer clicks onto mile 1.8.

1.8 Bear left and ease your way over a cut in the rocky lip where a rough jeep track drops north. Another singletrack detour goes right just after you drop over the lip. Then veer left to get back on the doubletrack (a singletrack goes right).

1.9 Doubletrack drops away on the left; stay straight at a three-way junction (with the shortcut mentioned at mile 0.5). Then bear left and stay on the level grade as another doubletrack jogs left and up to a small knob. Pedal north around the base of a grassy knob and stay straight where doubletrack falls away on the right.

2.0 Doubletrack crosses going up- and downhill. Go straight, looking out at St. Helena Cathedral, dead ahead. Follow the rocky singletrack that drops away left and into the trees. Loose and fixed rocks give parts of this section a -4 rating.

2.1 Break out in the open again on a knob overlooking the old limestone quarry above Second Street. Follow the doubletrack left down some limestone steps; the right branch goes to a steep drop—a great hillclimb test.

2.2 Turn right to drop between two grassy hills. (Staying left here leads to a rocky singletrack dropping west and around the north flank of the quarry hill. It joins the west end of Second Street.)

2.3 Bounce down to the rocky dead end of Chaucer Street, one block west of the Beattie Street Trailhead. Enjoy the downhill run back into town, watching for traffic at all intersections.

Mount Ascension Entertainment Loop

Location: In the South Hills, about 0.5 mile south of Broadway between Last Chance Gulch and the Capitol complex.

Distance: 5.1 miles.

Time: 40 minutes to 1.5 hours.

Tread: 1.3 miles on doubletrack; 2.3 miles on singletrack; 1.2 miles on gravel road; 0.3 mile on paved road.

Aerobic level: Strenuous going up Mount Ascension, but with a long downhill runout.

Technical difficulty: Mostly 3 to 3+, but several -5 sections on the climb. The downhill trail is 3+ to 4.

Hazards: Yield to other trail users; control your speed on descents.

Highlights: Great singletrack just beyond one of Helena's oldest neighborhoods. It's a first-class ridge ride with outstanding

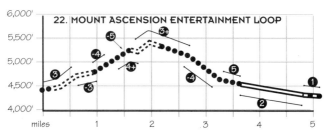

Mount Ascension Entertainment Loop

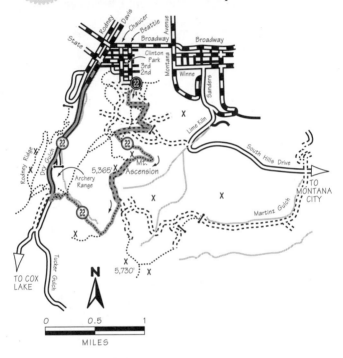

views of town and the North Hills, a rip-snortin' downhill, and a good chance of seeing deer and other wildlife.

Land status: Beattie Street City Park; private property; Helena National Forest. Much of the open space adjoining the old neighborhood is slated for a housing development. Landowners higher upslope also may limit or prohibit access. Obey all posted property lines; ask for permission before crossing private land.

Maps: USGS Helena.

Access: From Last Chance Gulch pedal east on Broadway about five blocks uphill to Rodney Street. Turn right on Rodney, pedal one long block south, and turn left onto State Street. Coast down to Davis, then climb again on State and continue three blocks east to Beattie. Turn right on Beattie and go uphill five blocks to where the road dead-ends by an open field. Total distance from Last Chance Gulch to the trailhead is 1.1 miles. The trail begins at the hiker's gate in the fence at road's end, which marks the boundary of Beattie Street Park.

The ride:

0.0   Ride through the gate and climb hard on singletrack. The trail eases off and contours into a small ravine at the treeline.

0.1   Drop into the gully and climb hard again. The trail bends left and levels off. Two less obvious singletracks go right here; stay straight.

0.2   Hop the kelly hump onto an old roadbed. Several trails branch right and uphill; pedal east on the road.

0.3   Doubletrack cuts across the roadbed (a challenging climb going right—it rejoins the route described here in 150 yards). The easiest route goes straight to meet a rough jeep track. Turn right and climb between ruts, going south toward Mount Ascension.

0.5   The road forks and a doubletrack comes in from the left and downhill. The right-hand fork climbs to a level grade and joins other trails on the northwest flank of Mount Ascension (see Ride 21). Stay on the main road as it veers left and continue the moderate climb. Ignore the next doubletrack in 50 feet, also on the right.

0.6 A gate straight ahead is posted against trespass. Follow the hairpin turn right onto a level grade and a boulder barricade. The landowner set these here to exclude motor vehicles. (As of this writing, land beyond the boulders was closed to all trespass without prior permission.) Look for an opening on the right if you've been given leave to enter. Resume climbing on the doubletrack, now headed west.

0.8 A gated private road comes in on the left; stay straight and continue climbing. In about 150 feet a singletrack drops off the bank above the road on the left, crosses the road, and plunges downhill into the trees on the right. Stay on the main road.

0.9 The grade eases onto a broad bench with sweeping views north and west. This is your last chance to take an easy swig from your water bottle; the climb gets serious from here. (See Ride 21 for easier options from this point.) Ignore the numerous doubletracks that fan out between 11 and 2 o'clock. Instead, make a sharp left around a green metal fencepost (a rocky doubletrack goes straight uphill to the big "C" on Mount Ascension here) and climb onto a faint singletrack going east into the trees. This trail soon begins climbing hard and never really lets up, but at least it's shady and smooth.

1.3 Break onto the ridge (a 3+ move) and bank right and uphill onto a wide, loose, rocky track that crawls directly up the hogback toward Mount A's summit. Limestone ledges alternate with loose gravel to challenge the traction-impaired. Everybody's thighs go to mush on this sustained uphill grind. This stretch is harder than it looks and rates a -5 for how rarely anyone rides it clean.

1.4 Crank over one last toothy chunk of bedrock (the crux move at a solid 5) and lean left on singletrack where old doubletrack shoots straight up the fall line. The singletrack contours south, then begins wrapping up and westward. There's one particularly steep, loose spot (where singletrack splits right and uphill at an impossibly steep rate). Pump through this (4+ for loose, sidesloped tread) and stay on the contour.

1.6 Join doubletrack running down Mount A's backside. The right branch leads up 20 yards to the first summit knob (at about 5,290 feet) and terrific views all around; the left goes down to start the ridge ride. Take it slow over the low rock ledges here (3+) and rattle south along the ridge.

1.7 Brief saddle; a doubletrack falls away on the right (it drops like an Escher staircase to Ride 21). Go straight and climb a set of limestone steps, following doubletrack south onto the open ridge.

1.8 Climb right over more bedrock—there's nothing harder than a 3+ between you and the second summit knob.

1.9 Enjoy another great vantage point from the top, at 5,365 feet. A fast downhill beckons to the south.

2.0 The runout ends on a jagged piece of hogback—notorious for shredding tires and tubes. Doubletrack drops left onto private property; stay straight on the ridge. The route rolls south through scattered trees and grassy clearings.

2.2 After swinging back into a few trees, the track dips left and right. Watch for a singletrack veering off to the right. Lean hard right to make the turn for the Entertainment run (or go straight on the doubletrack to continue the ridge ride; see Ride 23).

2.4 Smooth, sinuous singletrack breaks out of the trees into a vast meadow on the west flank of Mount Ascension Ridge. The tread is fairly narrow, so don't gawk at the scenery while you're rolling.

2.5 The trail dips into a wooded ravine then contours into another large, grassy clearing. The trail cuts across a steep slope and sidehills in a few spots, so watch your speed. Keep your uphill pedal high to avoid snagging it in the dirt.

2.6 Bank through another wooded gully.

2.7 As the trail enters a small clearing, watch for a singletrack dropping right; it's often hidden by tall grass. A large pine tree that forks into two big trunks marks the junction. Going straight ahead will lead you to a nice, grassy knoll followed by a bike-busting luge run through loose boulders on a 20 percent grade. So take the singletrack right instead, and zoom downhill into deep woods. To the right the trees fall away into a sharp ravine. Some of the drops ahead are deceptively steep—control your speed.

3.0 Juke through a shallow side gully and keep the nose pointed downhill.

3.2 The grade eases briefly, then dives downhill again.

3.3 Where the trees thin out a bit and the ravine runs farther off to the right, a well-disguised trail goes right and into the ravine. This spur links up with the Mount Ascension Lower Loop (Ride 21), a popular way back to town. For the official Entertainment exit, stay straight on the main trail for 50 feet and turn left at the next trail fork. Go another 50 feet across a rocky doubletrack, then follow the tire tracks downhill into an abrupt left turn (ignoring the old, eroded trail going straight downhill).

3.4 Coast into a brushy opening and hang on for a wild series of four switchbacks above Dry Gulch Road. All are tight and some shoot right down the fall line—a serious 5 for technical difficulty.

3.6   Watch for cars as you bottom out onto Dry Gulch Road (Ride 18). Hang a right and buzz back down to town. Be alert for washboards and traffic.

3.7   Entrance to the Lewis and Clark Archers' range (private and dangerous to boot) on right; stay on Dry Gulch Road.

4.8   As pavement begins, Dry Gulch Road becomes Davis Street. Cruise downhill. Smooth, ain't it?

5.0   Third Street goes right. If you left a vehicle at the Beattie Street trailhead, turn right here and pedal three blocks east to Beattie, then south three blocks to the trailhead (about 0.4 mile).

5.1   State Street. You're as good as home.

23

Mount Ascension Ridge Loop

Location: In the South Hills, about seven blocks south of Broadway between Last Chance Gulch and the Capitol complex.

Distance: 2.8 miles one way to uppermost knob on ridge; possible 8.5-mile open loop.

Time: 1 to 2 hours.

Tread: 3.3 miles on gravel road; 1.9 miles on paved road; 2.4 miles on doubletrack; 0.9 mile on singletrack.

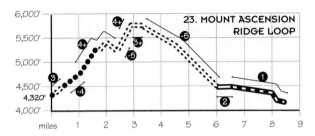

Aerobic level: Strenuous (!) going up, but with a long downhill runout.

Technical difficulty: Mostly 3, but several -5 sections on the climb; going downhill is 3+ to 4.

Hazards: Yield to other trail users; control your speed on descents. This exposed ridge is no place to be during a thunderstorm.

Highlights: A great singletrack right out one of Helena's oldest neighborhoods. The long ridge ride offers outstanding 360-degree views, a diabolic downhill, and a good chance of seeing deer and other wildlife.

Land status: Beattie Street City Park; private property; Helena National Forest. Much of the open space adjoining the old neighborhood is slated for a housing development. Landowners higher upslope also may limit access. Obey all posted property lines and ask for permission before crossing private land.

Maps: USGS Helena.

Access: From Last Chance Gulch pedal east on Broadway about five blocks uphill to Rodney Street. Turn right on Rodney, pedal one long block south, then turn left onto State Street. Coast down to Davis, then climb again on State and continue three blocks east to Beattie. Turn right on Beattie and go uphill five blocks to where the road dead-ends by an open field.

Total distance from Last Chance Gulch to the trailhead is 1.1 miles. The trail begins at the hiker's gate in the fence at road's end, which marks the boundary of Beattie Street Park.

The ride:

0.0 Ride through the gate and climb hard on singletrack. The trail eases off and contours into a small ravine at the treeline.

0.1 Drop into the gully and climb hard again. The trail bends left and levels. Two less obvious singletracks go right here; stay straight.

0.2 Hop the kelly hump onto an old roadbed. Several trails branch right and uphill; pedal east on the road.

0.3 A doubletrack cuts across the roadbed (a challenging climb going right—it rejoins the route described here in 150 yards). The easiest route goes straight to meet a rough jeep track. Turn right and climb between ruts, going south toward Mount Ascension.

0.5 The road forks and doubletrack comes in from the left and downhill. Stay on the main road as it veers left and continue the moderate climb. Ignore the next doubletrack (in 50 feet), also on the right.

0.6 A gate straight ahead is posted against trespass. Follow the hairpin turn right onto a level grade and a boulder barricade. The landowner adjusts these periodically to exclude motor vehicles. As of this writing public access was prohibited beyond these boulders without prior permission. If you've got it, look for an opening on the right. Resume climbing on the doubletrack, now headed west.

0.8 Gated private road on the left; stay straight and continue climbing. In about 150 feet a singletrack drops off

• Mount Ascension Ridge Loop

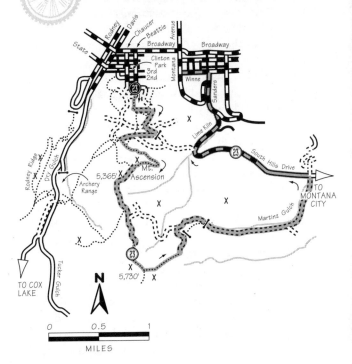

the left road bank, crosses the road, and plunges down-hill into the trees on the right. Stay on the main road.

0.9 The grade eases onto a broad bench with sweeping views north and west. This is your last chance to take an easy swig from your water bottle—the climb gets serious from here. (See Ride 21 for easier options from this point.) Ignore the numerous doubletracks that fan out between 11 and 2 o'clock. Instead, make a sharp left around a green metal fencepost (a rocky doubletrack goes straight uphill to the big "C" on Mount Ascension) and climb onto a faint singletrack going east into the trees. This smooth and shady trail soon begins climbing hard and never really lets up.

1.3 Break onto the ridge (3+) and bank right and uphill onto a wide, loose, rocky track that crawls directly up the hogback toward Mount A's summit. Limestone ledges alternate with loose gravel to challenge the traction-impaired. Feel your thighs go to mush on this sustained uphill grind. This stretch is harder than it looks and rates a -5 for how rarely anyone rides it clean.

1.4 Crank over one last toothy chunk of bedrock (the crux move at a solid 5) and lean left on singletrack where old doubletrack shoots straight up the fall line. The singletrack contours south, then begins wrapping up and westward. There's one particularly steep loose spot (where singletrack splits right and uphill at an impossibly steep rate); pump through this (4+ for loose, sidesloped tread) and stay on the contour.

1.6 Join doubletrack running down Mount A's backside. A right turn leads up 20 yards to the first summit knob (at about 5,290 feet) and terrific views all around; a left goes down to start the ridge ride. Take it slow over the low rock ledges here (3+) and rattle south along the ridge.

1.7 Brief saddle; doubletrack falls away on the right to Ride 21. Go straight and climb a set of limestone steps, following the doubletrack south onto the open ridge.

1.8 Climb right over more bedrock—nothing harder than a 3+.

1.9 Enjoy another great vantage point from the second summit knob (5,365 feet), but a fast downhill beckons, dropping south.

2.0 The runout ends on a jagged piece of hogback that's notorious for shredding tires and tubes. A doubletrack drops left onto private property; stay straight on ridge. The route rolls south through scattered trees and grassy clearings.

2.1 After swinging back into a few trees, the track dips left and right. Watch for singletrack veering off to the right (see Ride 22). To stay on the ridge, bear left on fading doubletrack and continue climbing south.

2.3 Jump on those pedals to climb out of the trees onto a knob of white limestone. The climb ahead rises along the grassy ridge at about 11 o'clock. Another doubletrack dives sharply to the left, dropping quickly to the Thompson-Nistler road cut. This is a good escape route if weather or darkness threaten, or if you're just tired of climbing. To continue the ridge climb, crank it south along the increasingly rocky doubletrack through a vast meadow. Four-wheelers sometimes drive off track here, but please stay on the main, established track to curtail erosion. Pick your way through the boulder maze—a solid 4 if you're accustomed to rock-hopping bowling balls, a 5 if this is new terrain.

2.5 Grade eases briefly. The track contours right and cuts across a low knob.

2.6 Drop onto the east flank of the ridge and enjoy a brief downhill. Gear down for the climb ahead—after a half-hour of climbing, you'll find out if you have any juice left! Favor the right or center tracks for the best traction.

2.8 Top of the hill! Follow the doubletrack left onto a level, grassy bench and spin out those quivering thighs. At 5,730 feet, you're 270 feet higher than Mount Helena and more than 1,600 feet above Last Chance Gulch.

To return to town, retrace your tracks (opting for the Entertainment Loop—Ride 22—for a change of scenery), or aim east on the doubletrack to reach the Thompson-Nistler Road. As homes are built up here, this leg of the loop may become off-limits to bikers and other wayfarers. Watch for "no trespassing" signs and don't cross private property without permission. The doubletrack drops east, then climbs northeast to a bald knob.

3.1 Recent dozer excavations rough up the tread near the top of the knob. Bear left (north), ignoring dozer tracks going right. The doubletrack bounces down the ridge over loose, rocky tread.

3.3 Drop left onto a fresh-cut dozer road and hang on as it plunges through several switchbacks into a gully. A gate blocks the bottom end by a new house. Go right when you land on the Thompson-Nistler Road. Cruise north and east on this hardpan (gumbo when wet).

4.3 Lean through a big looping left turn.

4.5 Dismount and walk under the metal gate. Remount, then beeline east and downhill into Martinz Gulch. Watch for pockets of loose gravel and deep ruts angling across the fall line.

5.8 South Hills Drive; watch for traffic. Turn left and pedal west (see Ride 24). The road climbs moderately at first, then levels off. Deer are common.

6.6 Pavement begins.

6.9 Begin descending into Lime Kiln Gulch. Bank around the big right turn and ease off the brakes for a fast sashay down Lime Kiln Road. Watch for traffic!

7.6 Watch for traffic turning east. Go straight.

7.8 Stop and look both ways before turning left onto Virginia Dale.

7.9   Harris Street drops away on right; stay straight on Virginia Dale.

8.0   Virginia Dale swings north and becomes Sanders. It's a paved downhill . . . this must be why some people still own road bikes. Watch for cross traffic at intersections.

8.2   Squeal the brakes for the stop sign at Illinois Street.

8.3   Junction with Winne Avenue. Go left four blocks to . . .

8.5   South Montana Avenue. Locals will know how to get home from here. If you left a vehicle at the trailhead on Beattie, drop north on Montana Avenue one block, turn left onto Third Street, and pedal west, zigzagging downhill and west whenever the streets dead-end against the hills ahead. When you reach Beattie Street, turn left and pedal uphill to the trailhead.

South Hills Drive Loop

Location: In the hills immediately southeast of Helena.

Distance: 9.1-mile loop.

Time: 1 to 2 hours.

Tread: 3.9 miles on paved road; 5.2 miles on gravel or dirt road.

Aerobic level: Easy.

Technical difficulty: 1 on paved roads; 2 to 2+ on gravel and dirt roads.

Hazards: Watch for traffic. Sections of Capitol Drive have large ruts and potholes.

Highlights: This easy road loop offers good views of Helena and the valley and a surprisingly good chance of seeing deer and pronghorn.

Land status: City of Helena and private property. Capitol Drive and South Hills Drive are private roads. Local residents pay for plowing, grading, and other maintenance. Both roads are posted as closed to non-resident motor vehicles, but to date cyclists and hikers have been allowed access. Future access is uncertain. Please stay on the designated route and heed all signs.

Maps: Helena National Forest; USGS Helena, East Helena.

Access: Begin this loop ride from the State Capitol area.

The ride:

0.0   Corner of Broadway and Montana Avenue. Pedal east on Broadway.

0.2   Stop sign at Sanders Street; continue straight on Broadway.

· South Hills Drive Loop

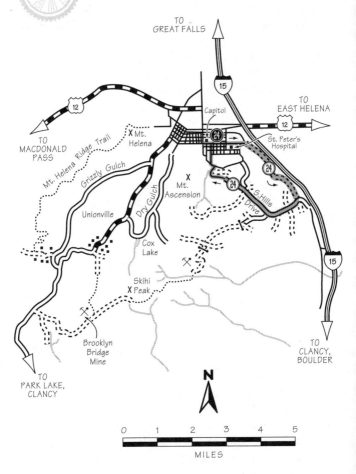

TO
GREAT FALLS

15

TO
EAST HELENA

12

Capitol

TO
MACDONALD
PASS

12

Mt. Helena Ridge Trail

X Mt.
Helena

Grizzly Gulch

Dry Gulch

24

St. Peter's
Hospital

24

X
Mt.
Ascension

24

S. Hills
Drive

Unionville

Cox
Lake

15

Skihi
X Peak

Brooklyn
Bridge
Mine

TO
CLANCY,
BOULDER

TO
PARK LAKE,
CLANCY

N

0   1   2   3   4   5

MILES

0.4	Pass the governor's house (at Carson Street) on the left.
0.5	Lockey Park on the left.
0.6	Stop sign at Lamborn Street; continue straight on Broadway.
1.1	Stop sign at California Street; continue straight on Broadway past St. Peter's Hospital on the right.
1.4	Turn right on Colonial Drive. Stay on Colonial as it curves left, leading away from town.
1.7	Pavement ends. A sign reads "Road Closed to Thru Traffic." Access for cyclists beyond this point is at the discretion of the landowners. Pedal east on the rough dirt road, which parallels Interstate 15.
1.9	Spur road goes right; stay straight.
2.2	Doubletrack hillclimb goes right; stay straight.
2.3	Doubletrack goes right; stay left.
2.6	Doubletrack joins from right; stay left.
2.9	Paradise Lane (private) goes right; stay straight.
3.0	Private drive on right.
3.3	Doubletrack goes up the slope ahead; bear left to stay on the main road. Before homes were built in this area, pronghorn were prevalent on these grassy hills.
3.5	Doubletrack goes right; stay straight on the main road as it drops into a small creek drainage.
3.6	Gear down for the only steep climb on this ride—it's short. The road levels off and passes several newer homes on the right.
3.8	Turn right onto South Hills Drive (a left leads to a paved road to East Helena and U.S. Highway 12). Stay on South Hills, climbing at an easy grade going southeast.
4.5	Junction with Quarry Road. A sign here prohibits "unauthorized motor vehicles" from using South Hills Drive. Cyclists, however, can keep pedaling as the road bends west.

5.1	Holmes Gulch Road goes left (see Ride 25); stay straight on South Hills Drive and dig into a long easy-to-moderate climb.
5.8	Enjoy a brief downhill.
5.9	Martinz Gulch Road goes left (see Ride 23). For a short-cut back to town, turn right here and take the next left, Tizer Road. It drops quickly (watch for washboards) to the east end of Saddle Drive and Gold Rush Avenue. To stay on the main route, climb west on South Hills and enjoy a nice view of the valley and mountains beyond.
6.1	The grade levels off.
6.9	Bump onto pavement.
7.1	Begin the descent into Lime Kiln Gulch.
7.3	Lean into a big right turn. From here the road snakes downhill through the gulch.
7.9	Watch for traffic turning into a private road on the right.
8.0	Turn left on Virginia Dale.
8.2	The road falls away to the right (north) and becomes Sanders Street. Watch for cross traffic on Ohio Avenue, midway down the hill.
8.4	Hit the brakes for the stop sign on Illinois Avenue. Continue north on Sanders.
8.6	Stop at Winne, then zigzag north to stay on Sanders.
8.9	Turn left on Broadway.
9.1	Corner of Broadway and Montana. A deli in the basement of the Capitol offers cold soda pop, sandwiches, and snacks.

Brooklyn Bridge Loop

Location: 8 miles south of Helena on the divide between Jefferson and Lewis and Clark counties.

Distance: 24.5-mile loop.

Time: 2.5 to 4.5 hours.

Tread: 7.1 miles on paved road; 7.6 miles on gravel road; 6 miles on doubletrack; 3.8 miles on singletrack.

Aerobic level: Strenuous, with long intervals at moderate grades. There are nine—count 'em—distinct climbs on the backcountry portion of this ride, all of them graded for granny gears. Riding the entire loop leaves most riders rubber-legged.

Technical difficulty: 1 and 2 on roads; 3 to 4+ on

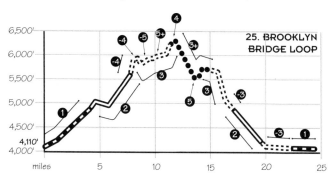

doubletrack. Occasional spots rate a solid 5 (boulder gardens, loose climbs).

Hazards: Watch for traffic on roads. Carry plenty of water and quick-energy snacks. Be prepared for changing weather and mechanical failures. This is a rough trail and help is a long way off.

Highlights: A marathon ride with a remote feel and the gamut of singletrack conditions—arduous climbs, sweet downhills, boulder gardens, logs to bunny hop, bog crossings, sidehills, and route-finding riddles. A fair chance of seeing deer, elk, black bear, and other wildlife.

Land status: Helena National Forest; Bureau of Land Management; private property. Portions of this ride traverse private holdings, some of which may be posted against trespass. Please heed all posted property boundaries. Also, the USDA Forest Service may regarde some long-abandoned roads as part of a proposed "vegetation manipulation" project. Future access is uncertain.

Maps: Helena National Forest; USGS Helena.

Access: If you've got the time and energy, do this as a loop starting and ending in town at the City-County Building. To reduce the distance (and overall climbing), drive to the actual trailhead at mile 7.5 in the description below and arrange a shuttle after the ride.

The ride:

0.0 From the City-County Building on Park Avenue pedal south on Park, which becomes the Orofino Gulch or Unionville Road as it leaves town.

Brooklyn Bridge Loop

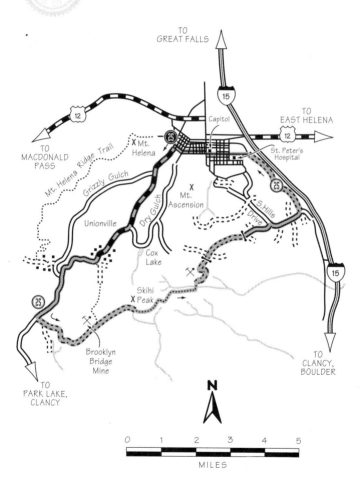

1.0 Grizzly Gulch splits right; stay on pavement going left. The ride south to Unionville is a steady moderate climb, with slightly steeper grades where Dry Gulch Estates Road comes in and at the final approach to Unionville.

3.9 Welcome to downtown Unionville, where the dogs are friendly and the traffic slows to 25 mph.

4.4 Pavement ends. Continue climbing on the dusty gravel road.

4.5 Grade eases; enjoy a brief downhill run.

5.6 Resume climbing at a moderate clip.

5.8 Grizzly Gulch Road goes right (see Ride 9). Instead, go straight, following signs pointing south for Park Lake. The road narrows and traffic thins beyond here, but be wary on blind curves. And don't expect to hurry up the grade—it gains 1,000 feet in the next 1.7 miles. Most riders consider this stretch strenuous.

7.5 The road tops out at the Orofino–Lump Gulch Divide. Turn left and cross a cattleguard onto rough doubletrack leading east into the trees. All warmed up? The real climbing starts here. The first pitch (Climb One) is just a warm-up, with a deep erosion gully and loose, sidehilled tread. It's even steeper near the top. Go for it.

7.7 Climb One tops out at a three-way junction. Doubletrack going right leads 50 yards to a viewpoint over Lump Gulch. The middle track is signed as Forest Road 4010-B1. Take the left doubletrack that drops east into an open forest. Hang on for a sandy banked left turn, then level tread. From here on out the main route is marked with tree blazes doused in red paint.

7.9 The doubletrack forks; the right-hand track is the way to go but it's usually blocked by a mud hole. Skirt the puddle on the left and get ready to climb.

8.0 Gear down for Climb Two, one of the rockier, steeper pitches. Some riders prefer attacking this from the left-hand doubletrack back at mile 7.9; it joins the climb at the midway point. Either way is rideable, a -4 due to loose babyhead rocks.

8.1   Climb Two tops out. A grassy doubletrack goes right; stay left.

8.2   Grassy doubletrack goes left; stay right and drop down a steep, mildly rocky pitch. The route forks here— either way works.

8.3   The forks rejoin and the grade levels off in open lodge-pole forest. Bank right (south) and enjoy a long, gentle downhill run.

8.6   Slow for a boggy spot, best skirted on the right.

8.8   Doubletrack goes right. The main route curves left and uphill, beginning Climb Three. Favor the right-hand track at first, then meander as needed. It gets rockier and steeper (with a dose of -5) near the top.

9.1   Top of Climb Three. The trail falls away gently (stay left where doubletrack goes right), running on pine needles and occasional rocks. It's bouncy at higher speeds.

9.2   Doubletrack goes left; stay right. There's no easy way to avoid the next boggy section, but it's short. Then the trail cuts left and drops to a small clearing.

9.4   Lean left again for a 90-degree turn (a faint doubletrack goes right). The road winds between lodgepole on the right and aspen on the left.

9.6   The track forks. Go left.

9.4   A faded doubletrack goes left; the main route curves right and begins Climb Four. The uphill side offers a fairly clean (level 3) line.

9.7   Climb Four tops out. A thin doubletrack goes right, but you lean left and roll through the lodgepoles on a level run.

9.8   Let 'er loose on a short downhill.

10.1 Lean left and skirt another boggy area, then pedal up a moderate grade.

10.2 Scan the boulder garden ahead for a rideable line, but don't expect it to last more than 10 feet. Lots of folks just walk these 60 yards of "trail." Skilled riders can pop it into low gear and enjoy a slow-motion rodeo through the obstacle course. It's a 5+, but rideable if you don't panic when you run out of route options.

10.3 Climb easily to a small, grassy clearing above the Brooklyn Bridge Mine. Forest Road 4010-C1 drops north from here (behind the sign), offering a steep shortcut (crossing private property) back to Unionville. A landowner on the Unionville end of FR 4010-C1 has at times used force to prohibit trespassing, but more and more folks are riding it. Swing right to stay on the main route.

10.6 After an easy run, begin climbing moderately.

10.8 Grade steepens into Climb Five, which eases slightly after an initial grunt.

10.9 Climb hard out of the trees on grassy wheel ruts.

11.1 Climb Five levels off at about 6,280 feet in a U-shaped meadow where the tracks fork. Turning left leads uphill (steep!) and north along a grassy ridge for 0.3 mile, offering decent views east and south. The main route goes right (sometimes hidden by tall grass), dropping below a stand of aspen, then diving right into the pines again.

11.2 Several side trails fall away on right; stay left on a more gradual descent. Bank for a hard right turn.

11.3 Join doubletrack coming in from the right. Lean left and drop into a steep, rocky chute (a solid 4 unless you actually enjoy nose wheelies). Clear the rocky spot and bank left on singletrack that skirts an aspen-choked meadow. The trail is mostly singletrack for the next 3.8 miles.

11.5 Singletrack climbs left; stay right.

11.6 Cut left and gear down for Climb Six, rated 3+ but strenuous.

11.8 Top of Climb Six.

12.0 The trail sweeps left along a trackless meadow with views south toward Boulder Hill. Then it drops into a twisty, banked descent that widens into doubletrack. As it falls away and grows rockier, favor the right-hand track.

12.4 Give your hands a rest as the grade eases and the tread runs smooth and wide. The trail zips through lodgepole and a carpet of grouse whortleberry just right of a grassy, aspen-lined creek bottom.

12.9 Slow for a sharp left turn (a rough track cuts right and uphill here). Drop into the tall grass of the creek bottom and watch for hidden boulders and branches. The trail goes left and backtracks west along the opposite side of the creek.

13.0 Climb through a right turn full of rocks back into the lodgepoles.

13.1 Begin Climb Seven—the shortest, but one of the hardest to ride clean. It's steep and full of roots and rocks, a 5 for most riders.

13.2 Take a short breather as the trail levels off, then jumps into Climb Eight, the longest pitch. Gradual at first, it shoots for the sky at mile 13.4. Keep that rear tire digging.

13.6 Climb Eight eases off in the smallest of clearings (riders collapsing on the ground probably keep seedlings from taking over). From here the trail drops left into a lodgepole hallway.

13.9 Hike your bike through yet another aspen bog. Tall grass hides holes, rocks, logs—and the trail, too. Aim straight across; an obvious trail takes off from the far side (and is rumored to empty out in Tucker Gulch, at the head of Dry Gulch) but don't pedal down it. Instead, look right for a red blaze and a faint grassy tread winding into the lodgepoles. Follow this track, which quickly becomes better defined and runs down another hallway in the pines. Expect lots of rocks and pole-sized downfall.

14.2 Roll left and downhill.

14.4 Enter a grassy aspen stand, curve right past an old, roofless cabin, then drop through a twisty section that ends in a 4+ jumble of rocks. From here enjoy a long stretch of fast, gradual descent.

14.7 Pass a stack of slanted boulders on the left, detouring around a downed log that's been here for years, and hum through more smooth running (with a few minor bouncy spots).

15.1 Join doubletrack on an old roadbed winding north.

15.4 Climb Nine is short but rocky and loose in parts, a 4+. The drop down the other side is easier. Lean right at the bottom.

15.5 A well-defined doubletrack breaks onto an open hillside overlooking Montana City and Strawberry Mountain to the east. The stacks at East Helena's smelter rise from the valley straight ahead. Watch for pockets of deep sand in the tread.

15.7 Drop into a bulldozed mining area. Doubletrack goes right; stay left.

15.8 Switchback left.

15.9 Slow for a sandy switchback right. Keep switchbacking, ignoring the spur roads at the apex of each turn. Be alert for loose sand, rocks, and deep erosion gullies.

16.2 A fenceline marks private property. This is sometimes posted. To date, cyclists have been allowed to pass here. Please close the gate.

16.3 The road drops into a broad cattle pasture, usually occupied. Watch for fresh cow pies. A lone Douglas-fir shows a red blaze on its trunk; pedal toward the tree, then go right along wheel tracks through the grass. The open slope above and to the northwest is the backside of Mount Ascension (see Ride 23). Stay on the wheel tracks in the open pasture. They grow more obvious as the track runs northeast and down toward the creek.

16.7 Drop down a rocky section, back into the trees. The track forks; go right, along the creek bottom. The doubletrack soon crosses the creek then careens downhill over thank-you-ma'am dips and bumps.

16.9 Singletrack goes right and climbs; stay straight on doubletrack.

17.3 Second fenceline. The gate here was strung extra tight with new wire in August 1996, making it easier to pass a bike and body through the fence than to wrestle with the gate. If you do open the gate, please close it behind you. Pedal north on gravel Holmes Gulch Road.

17.5 A side road climbs right; stay straight.

18.1 Timber Lane goes left; stay straight.

18.5 Junction with South Hills Drive. Go left for the shortest route back to town (see Ride 24). To finish the standard loop go right on South Hills.

18.7 Ponderosa Road goes right; stay straight.

19.1 Quarry Road crosses your path; stay straight.

19.5 Sky Line Drive goes right; stay straight.

19.7 Pronghorn Road goes left; stay straight. In 50 yards turn left on gravel Capitol Drive, which parallels Interstate 15, running northwest.

19.9 Drop hard into a swale and climb the other side.

20.1 Round a turn and shift into that big chainring for the long contour into town.

20.6 Paradise Lane (private drive) goes left. Other roads and doubletracks split off the main route. Some are tempting hillclimbs, but all cross private land. Please stay off all posted property.

21.8 Bounce onto pavement—the east end of Colonial Drive.

22.0 Turn left onto Broadway and climb moderately, heading west.

22.2 Turn left at St. Peter's Hospital if you can't ride any farther. Or continue west on Broadway 2.2 miles to Park Avenue, then go 0.1 mile north to the City-County Building to close the loop.

Black Hall Meadows Loop

Location: From town and back, through the mountains at the head of Colorado Gulch 10 miles southwest of Helena.

Distance: 33-mile loop.

Time: 2.5 to 4 hours.

Tread: 13.9 miles on paved road; 15.6 miles on gravel road; 3.5 miles on double- and singletrack.

Aerobic level: Strenuous, though the backcountry sections are mostly moderate.

Technical difficulty: 1 to 2+ on paved and gravel roads; mostly 3 with sections of 4 on double- and singletrack.

Hazards: Watch for traffic on all open roads and downfall on trails and doubletrack. The route tops out on a 6,800-foot windblown ridge—carry a windshell or rain jacket. Also take extra water and a snack.

Highlights: This is a fairly non-technical ride with a wonderful, remote feel. Black Hall Meadows look like a sea of grass after riding through miles of dark forest. There's a good chance of seeing wildlife, including elk. Optional ride to the summit of Colorado Mountain (see Ride 27).

Land status: Helena National Forest and private property. Portions of this ride traverse private holdings, some of which may be posted against trespass. Please heed all posted property boundaries. Future access is uncertain.

Maps: Helena National Forest; USGS Helena, Black Mountain, Chessman Reservoir, MacDonald Pass.

Access: Ride from town or drive to the trailhead following the route described to mile 10.9 below (and see Ride 27). This loop can also be ridden in reverse, or done with a vehicle shuttle between the North Fork of Travis Creek Trailhead and Rimini Road (with ample parking at the Minnehaha Road junction or Tenmile Picnic Area).

The ride:

0.0 From the City-County Building on Park Avenue, pedal south on Park, which becomes the Orofino Gulch or Unionville Road as it leaves town.

1.0 Grizzly Gulch splits right; stay on pavement going left. The ride south to Unionville is a steady moderate climb, with slightly steeper grades where Dry Gulch Estates Road comes in and at the final approach to Unionville.

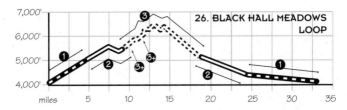

26. BLACK HALL MEADOWS LOOP

3.9 Welcome to downtown Unionville, where the dogs are friendly and the traffic slows to 25 mph.

4.4 Pavement ends. Continue climbing on the dusty gravel road.

4.5 Grade eases; enjoy a brief downhill run.

5.6 Resume climbing at a moderate clip.

5.8 Grizzly Gulch Road goes right (see Ride 9). Instead, go straight, following signs pointing south for Park Lake. The road narrows and traffic thins beyond here, but be wary on blind curves. And don't expect to hurry up the grade—it gains 1,000 feet in the next 1.7 miles. Most riders consider this stretch strenuous.

7.5 The road tops out at the Orofino–Lump Gulch Divide. A forest service road goes left at a cattle guard (see Ride 25). Stay on the main road and drop into a fast downhill run south. Watch for washboards, ruts, loose gravel, and well-anchored chucks of bedrock poking up from the tread.

8.3 A brown sign warns of the upcoming right turn onto the North Fork of Travis Creek Road (Forest Road 137). Ignore the doubletrack going left. Bank right and continue downhill. The North Fork Travis Creek Road quickly narrows to one-lane, lined with trees, as it skirts a cabin and grassy pasture on the left.

8.7 The grade levels out; gear down for the steep climb immediately ahead.

Black Hall Meadows Loop

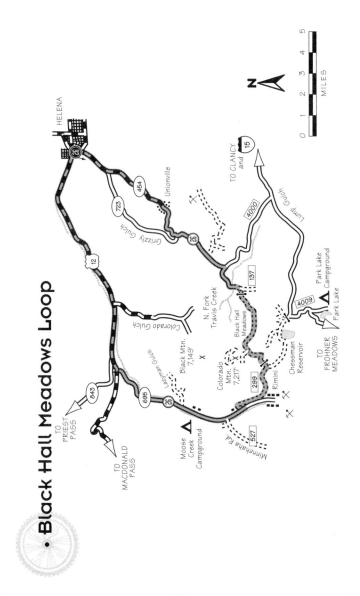

8.9 A private drive goes left; bend right with the main road as it tops out and eases off above another large pasture. Ignore several driveways on the right.

9.4 Two wider driveways go right; stay on main road as it banks left and downhill.

9.6 The road drops to a sandy, sometimes boggy spot, then bucks hard uphill and into the forest. The grade becomes strenuous, on often loose, rutted tread.

9.8 The road forks; go right.

9.9 Doubletrack climbs right, into the trees. Stay left on the main road.

10.2 Climb out of the forest onto an open ridge with good views east and south to the Elkhorns and west to Red Mountain. The grade levels off, then coasts downhill.

10.3 A doubletrack goes right; stay left.

10.7 A gated doubletrack goes right; stay left and drop to another low, sandy spot. Gear down for a moderate grunt, back into a lodgepole forest.

10.9 The road continues through an obvious turnaround area. A homemade sign reads "Dead End;" look for a Forest Service sign listing travel restrictions on the right. This marks the trailhead for Black Hall Meadows. The fence beyond looks continuous, but it actually overlaps, with a bikeable opening between the two sections. A clover-covered doubletrack leads from the road to the fence opening. Most folks count on an hour or more to ride to this point. If you drive, park off the road to one side of the turnaround.

Once on the trail, pedal west and uphill. The tread follows an old roadbed at a moderate pitch.

11.1 Scramble through a short rocky patch as the road bends right, then left.

11.2 The grade eases by a stand of aspen, then runs west through a pine forest.

11.4 Resume moderate climbing.

11.6 The grade levels then runs downhill through a small clearing.

11.7 Another uphill, on a well-defined singletrack bedded in the old road corridor.

11.9 Gear down for another rocky spot (rating 3+).

12.0 The trail climbs into a meadow, then curls downhill on smooth tread.

12.1 Slow for an abrupt ditch running across the tread. Then speed on downhill as the trail braids like an old cowpath back and forth across the grassy roadbed. Some sections here may be boggy, especially in spring and early summer or after rain.

12.4 A faint doubletrack backtracks left and uphill (worth exploring, anyone?). Stay on the main track as it bends right.

12.5 Roll along the edge of the trees into the widening expanse of lower Black Hall Meadows. Aspen rim the east edge, and midmeadow willows may hide moose or elk. The old road cuts directly across the meadows, with views west to Colorado Mountain and south, where Red Mountain hulks in its own shadow.

12.8 Put it into tractor mode as the trail contours hard left and uphill across the base of Colorado Mountain. The first pitch is often loose and sandy, with fist-sized rocks thrown in for fun. It's strenuous but no worse than a 3+.

13.0 Stop at the fenceline, and, as the sign says, "Please close the gate" behind you. Continue climbing; the top is in sight.

13.1 Roll into upper Black Hall Meadows. A wooden post on the left marks the junction with the doubletrack route to Colorado Mountain on the right (see Ride 27). The main trail curves left (south), edging between the forest and the linear meadow that follows this 6,800-foot ridge. Find a sunny spot with views of Red Mountain for a picnic, or sneak into the trees to get out of the ever-blasting wind, and take a well-deserved rest. You're a hammerhead if you made it here in less than 1.5 hours.

13.5 The trail splits. Left goes uphill toward Chessman Reservoir; stay right and drop onto a doubletrack that falls off the ridge into a steep draw above Beaver Creek.

13.7 Bank right through a switchback turn.

13.8 Bank left.

14.0 Tall grass marks a boggy spot and a metal culvert slants across the trail. From here the tread hugs the left side of the drainage bottom, just inside the forest edge.

14.3 A fenceline and gate. Tall grass often conceals the tread immediately below the gate. Bear left and onto singletrack that humps around a sudden sinkhole. This trail soon splits into parallel tracks. One breaks right and runs on the old roadbed in the grass (sometimes swamped by the creek). If that route is wet, stay on the left-hand track, which bounces over roots and between trees on higher ground. This drier track rejoins the main route in about 70 yards.

14.4 Back to civilization. Turn right onto one-lane, gravel Forest Road 299 and follow Beaver Creek (the outlet from Chessman Reservoir) as it dives to Tenmile Creek.

15.1 Tighten that helmet as the road falls away, dancing on rocks and washboards.

15.9 The grade eases briefly, then swoops downhill again. Watch for fallen rocks on the inside track of this one-lane road, and try to avoid kiting off the lip if you favor the outer track.

17.0 Lean into a big left turn above a scattering of buildings.

17.2 Stop and look for traffic before turning right on the Rimini Road ("town" is just 1 mile away, to the left).

Expect fast traffic, washboards, and lungs full of dust for the next 6.3 miles. At least it's all downhill.

17.8 Minnehaha Road (FR 527) goes left; stay straight.

19.5 Moose Creek Campground on left.

19.9 Tenmile Picnic Area on right.

21.5 National forest boundary.

23.5 Turn right and ease those saddle sores onto paved U.S. Highway 12. A tailwind is almost guaranteed, the shoulder is wide, and it's 10 miles downhill to Helena.

31.8 Turn right onto Joslyn and pedal uphill 3 blocks. Turn left on Knight and crank it into town, watching for cross traffic at intersections.

33.0 Turn right onto Dearborn and pedal south 10 blocks to close the loop at the City-County Building, or kick it on home from here.

Colorado Mountain Pilgrimage

Location: 10 miles southwest of Helena, at the head of Colorado Gulch.

Distance: 3.5 miles one way.

Time: 45 minutes to 1.5 hours one way.

Tread: 3.5 miles on double- and singletrack.

Aerobic level: Strenuous, but not a gear-jammer.

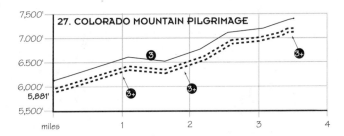

Technical difficulty: Mostly 3 with a few sections of 3+.

Hazards: Carry a windshell or rain jacket to cut the wind and chill at higher elevations. Cancel this ride if lightning threatens.

Highlights: This wide, shady trail has a remote feel despite signs of cattle grazing and past mining activity. Look for elk and deer, especially near vast Black Hall Meadows. Then enjoy a strenuous but fully rideable climb to the 7,217-foot bald knob of Colorado Mountain and outstanding views. Local mountain bikers should do this ride at least once a year.

Land status: Helena National Forest.

Maps: Helena National Forest; USGS Chessman Reservoir, Black Mountain.

Access: To drive to the trailhead from Helena go south on Park Avenue, which becomes Orofino Gulch or Unionville Road as it leaves town. Stay on this paved road 4 miles south to Unionville, then continue south where the road changes to good gravel. The upper end of Grizzly Gulch Road comes in from the right about 5.8 miles from town. Continue straight south here, following the signs for Park Lake. The road narrows and winds to the top of the Orofino–Lump Gulch Divide at mile 7.5. Continue down the road 0.8 mile and turn right onto the signed North Fork Travis Creek Road. Stay on this one-lane dirt road as it winds 2.6 miles south and west (and up and down) to an obvious turnaround spot marked by a homemade

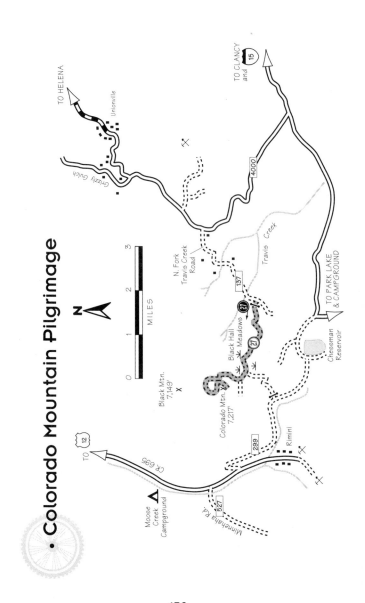

Colorado Mountain Pilgrimage

TO HELENA

Unionville

Grizzly Gulch

TO CLANCY and [15]

N

MILES

0 1 2 3

Black Mtn. 7,149'

N. Fork Travis Creek Road

Travis Creek

4000

137

29

27

Black Hall Meadows

Colorado Mtn. 7,217'

TO PARK LAKE & CAMPGROUND

Chessman Reservoir

[12]

TO

CR 696

Moose Creek Campground

Minnehaha Rd.

527

299

Rimini

"Dead End" sign. Much of this land is private, with no official public access despite some scattered Forest Service markers. The trail begins here, just beyond the fence to the right. Park off the road to one side of the turnaround.

More devout mountain bikers may want to ride from town, adding 10.9 miles (one way), about 1,600 feet of climbing, and at least an hour of pedaling to the ride described below. See Ride 26 for a description of the ride from town to the trailhead.

The ride:

0.0   Look for a Forest Service sign listing travel restrictions on the right. This marks the trailhead for Black Hall Meadows. The fence beyond looks continuous, but it actually overlaps, with a bikeable opening between the two sections. A clover-covered doubletrack leads from the road to the fence opening.

Once on the trail, pedal west and uphill. The tread follows an old roadbed at a moderate pitch.

0.2   Scramble through a short rocky patch as the road bends right, then left.

0.3   The grade eases by a stand of aspen, then runs west through pine forest.

0.5   Resume moderate climbing.

0.7   The grade levels, then runs downhill through a small clearing.

0.8   Uphill again, on a well-defined singletrack bedded in the old road corridor.

1.0   Gear down for another rocky spot—a 3+ on the technical scale.

1.1   The trail climbs into a meadow, then curls downhill on smooth tread.

1.2 Slow for an abrupt ditch across the tread. Then speed on downhill as the trail braids like an old cowpath back and forth across the grassy roadbed. Some sections here may be boggy, especially in spring and early summer or after rain.

1.5 A faint doubletrack backtracks left and uphill (worth exploring, anyone?). Stay on the main trail as it bends right.

1.6 Roll along the edge of the trees into the widening expanse of Black Hall Meadows. Aspens rim the east edge, and midmeadow willows may hide moose or elk. The old road cuts directly across the meadow, with views west to Colorado Mountain and south, where Red Mountain hulks in its own shadow.

1.9 Put it into tractor mode as the trail contours hard left and uphill across the base of Colorado Mountain. The first pitch is often loose and sandy, with fist-sized rocks thrown in for fun. It's strenuous but no worse than a 3+.

2.1 Pass through a gate, and close it behind you. Continue climbing.

2.2 Roll into upper Black Hall Meadows. Just as you break free of the trees a wooden post on the left marks the junction with the doubletrack route to Colorado Mountain on the right. Slam into granny gear (if you're not there already) and pedal north on the grassy doubletrack climbing the open slope.

2.3 A faint doubletrack goes left; stay right, climbing hard onto a more defined dirt track that ducks through a scattering of trees.

2.5 The grade eases onto the east flank of the mountain. Enjoy 30 yards of downhill.

2.6 The track seems to end in a grassy bowl, but look left and follow a big switchback turn to resume climbing. The doubletrack immediately switchbacks right, out of the trees and back onto the open ridge going north. The views here begin to hint at what awaits on top. Suck air and do penance as the mildly rocky track climbs through sagebrush and bunchgrass.

2.9 The grade eases again onto the mountain's forested east flank. The track contours north, climbing moderately.

3.0 Pause for an eagle-eye view to the right of Black Hall Meadows. Large downfall is common on this section of trail, and riders may have to dismount or detour off the roadbed. The climb continues at a moderate-to-easy grind.

3.3 Curve left around the north face of the mountain and gear down for a slightly steeper pitch onto the summit ridge, pedaling south now as the road coils in a nearly concentric circle.

3.4 Continue left onto the summit ridge, then follow the doubletrack right (south) as it bumps over large rocks and ruts.

3.5 Spin onto the bouldery, open summit, marked by concrete anchors for the lookout tower that once stood here. This is a great picnic spot, replete with 360-degree views. Chessman Reservoir sparkles to the south, beneath Red Mountain's broad hump. Look east to the Elkhorn Mountains, northeast to the distant Big Belts, and west to the Continental Divide. At 7,217 feet, Colorado Mountain is 900 feet higher than MacDonald Pass, visible to the northwest. Beyond the pass, the Nevada Creek basin slants toward the peaks lining the Seeley–Swan corridor.

When you've had your fill of scenery, retrace your tracks to the Black Hall Meadows trail and east to the trailhead; it takes about the same amount of time as the trip up. For other loop options, see Ride 26.

Head Lane to Scratchgravel Peak

Location: 6 miles north of Helena on the west end of the Helena Valley.

Distance: 8.1 miles one way.

Time: 1 to 3 hours.

Tread: 2.8 miles on paved road; 3.6 miles on gravel road; 1.2 miles on doubletrack; 0.5 mile on singletrack.

Aerobic level: Moderate to strenuous.

Technical difficulty: 1 on paved and gravel roads; 2+ to -4 on doubletrack; 3 to -4 on singletrack (but several steep grades require walking for all but superhuman riders).

Hazards: Watch for traffic on all roads. Stay on established roads and trails; these soils erode easily and prickly pear cacti are abundant. Expect flat tires if you wander off-trail. Ride in

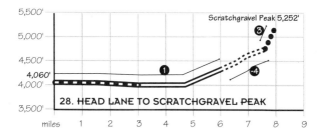

control and be alert for sand traps, ruts, slippery sidehills, and off-camber turns. In summer, carry extra water.

Highlights: The Scratchgravels are the place to ride when Helena's South Hills are muddy or snow closes the higher elevations. Scant precipitation and sandy soils mean dry trails and a longer riding season, even through winter in some years. There's also plenty of beginner and intermediate terrain, though the final hillclimb to the peak is for strong, skilled riders only. Anyone can enjoy the ride to a scenic overlook at mile 7.6, and many other trails beckon along the way. Watch for deer and birds of prey.

Land status: Bureau of Land Management and private property. Portions of this ride traverse private holdings, some of which may be posted against trespass. Please heed all posted property boundaries. Future access is uncertain.

Maps: Helena National Forest; USGS Scratchgravel Hills.

Access: This ride starts in town, requiring about 6.5 miles of road riding to reach BLM land in the Scratchgravels. Riders who prefer driving to the trailhead should use Echo Lane (see Ride 30), the only official public access to the Scratchgravels' interior. Please do NOT drive out Head Lane—cars parked at the end of Head Lane have been ticketed and towed at the owners' expense.

The ride:

0.0 From the Civic Center at the corner of Benton and Neill, pedal one block north and turn west on Hauser Boulevard.

1.3 Turn right on Joslyn Street and coast downhill.

1.5 Cross Euclid Avenue (U.S. Highway 12) at a traffic

Head Lane to
Scratchgravel Peak

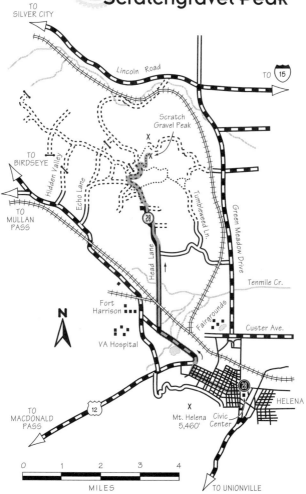

TO
SILVER CITY

TO 15

Lincoln Road

Scratch
Gravel Peak

X

X

TO
BIRDSEYE

Hidden Valley

Echo Lane

Tumbleweed Ln.

28

Head Lane

Green Meadow Drive

TO
MULLAN
PASS

Tenmile Cr.

Fort
Harrison

Fairgrounds

Custer Ave.

VA Hospital

N

28

HELENA

12

TO
MACDONALD
PASS

X
Mt. Helena
5,460'

Civic
Center

0   1   2   3   4

MILES

TO UNIONVILLE

164

light. Continue north on Joslyn for two blocks, then lean left to stay on the main paved road where Joslyn goes straight and becomes gravel. You're now on Country Club Road.

2.2 Pass Spring Meadow Lake State Park on the left (swimming, fishing, boating, picnic shelters, restrooms, fee area).

2.5 Archie Bray Foundation for the Ceramic Arts on left.

2.8 Turn right onto gravel Head Lane (the first right after the Bray Foundation; it's signed).

3.3 Cross railroad tracks.

4.1 A bridge crosses Sevenmile Creek. Begin climbing moderately.

4.7 Franklin Mine Road goes right; continue climbing north on Head Lane. Many private roads and driveways branch off during the next 1.6 miles, but all dead-end on private land. A sign on the right here reads: "Private Road—No BLM Access." To date, cyclists have not been denied access to BLM lands from the end of Head Lane, but this could change. Please stay on the main road and respect all posted property lines. Motorists should use Echo Lane (see Ride 31) for access.

6.2 Treeline Trail (a private road) goes right. Stay straight and pedal into a cul-de-sac. A driveway with a house number (6425) goes right at about 1 o'clock; head for the sandy road at high noon.

6.3 A private driveway forks left (look ahead to see numerous warning signs). Veer onto the right-hand fork—a jeep road—and gear down for a short, sandy climb through a left turn. Ignore the fading doubletrack going right.

6.4 Stop at the BLM map and information sign to get oriented. Another doubletrack goes right just beyond the sign; stay straight on the main jeep road.

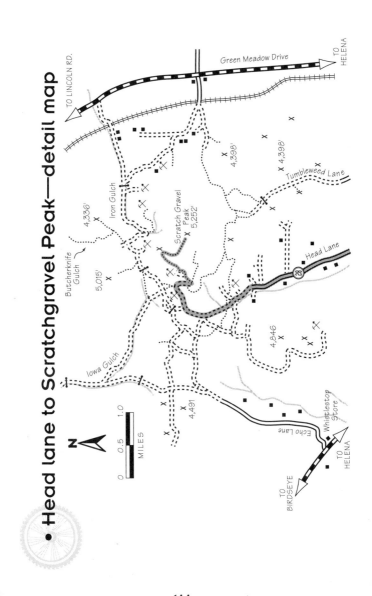

• Head lane to Scratchgravel Peak—detail map

Green Meadow Drive

TO LINCOLN RD.

TO HELENA

Butcherknife Gulch

Iron Gulch

4,336'

5,015'

Scratch Gravel Peak
5,252'

4,398'

4,398'

Tumbleweed Lane

Head Lane

28

Iowa Gulch

4,846

4,491

Echo Lane

Whistlestop Store

TO HELENA

TO BIRDSEYE

N

MILES

0   0.5   1.0

6.6 A doubletrack forks left, then another goes right. Left leads up a mostly moderate climb to a low spur ridge and a road that rejoins our route at mile 6.9 below. The other right track fades out in the sagebrush and prickly pear uphill. Stay on the main (center) jeep track, which turns rockier and steeper as it heads northwest. In 60 yards a singletrack blazes across the road; this is the trail described in Ride 29.

6.7 Begin a moderately strenuous climb over loose rocks and chunks of bedrock. The grade eases after a little more than 0.1 mile, then rolls past an old mineshaft on the left.

6.9 Roll into Head Lane junction, an intersection of jeep roads. If you opted for the easier climb going left at mile 6.6, welcome back to the described route. Straight (west) and downhill here leads to Echo Lane. Turn right and pedal uphill at a moderate clip over several rocky patches.

7.1 Jeep road goes left; stay right. The track becomes more sandy and rolls northeast and into the trees.

7.3 Ride through a rocky, deeply eroded section that marks the beginning of more strenuous climbing. Stay to the right where the track frays into several tracks going left and keep climbing. The route narrows as erosion gullies cut across the tread.

7.5 A cairn and colored flagging sometimes mark a thin singletrack going right and downhill. This is the start for the Scratchgravel Singletrack (Ride 29). Instead, stay on the jeep road and climb through a brief rocky, rutted section (rated -4).

7.6 The climb eases into a cul-de-sac with a lone tree in the middle. Had enough climbing? Park your bike by the tree and walk south to the pile of rocks. Scramble up the pile for a sunny perch overlooking Head Lane and the Broadwater area west of Helena. This makes a good turnaround point for most riders. Retrace your tire tracks to return to town. Be careful on the descent, and watch for sandy, sidesloped tread.

Diehards who want to reach Scratchgravel Peak should grab those bar ends and grind hard to the left and uphill (it's steep!). Figure on about 10 minutes of hard oxygen debt to reach the top from here.

Ignore the unmaintained, rock-strewn trail that switchbacks east from the cul-de-sac; it's a mess. Not that the main route is much better. Stay on the uphill side to avoid the rocky erosion gully. The track curves up and right.

7.7   The grade eases briefly; a doubletrack goes left 60 yards to an old mineshaft and tailing apron (with great views west). Stay right and keep climbing.

7.8   The trail narrows and arcs upward and right. This loose, rocky switchback can be ridden clean only on a helium-filled bike with suction-cup tires and Jor-el from planet Krypton in the saddle. The rest of us can get off and push uphill 'til we can remount and pedal again. The trail corkscrews through two more killer turns. If you're walking you can pause to enjoy glimpses east to the Big Belt Mountains.

7.9   Pedal onto a short flat spot—the beginning of the summit ridge—but hold onto your momentum for the loose, rocky pitch just ahead. From here the tread remains a narrow, sometimes rocky singletrack threading through wind-bent trees.

8.0   Dip right, then climb left on an easier grade through a small rock garden (a -4 if that rattle in your lungs doesn't shake you off the bike).

8.1   Scramble up two sets of bedrock steps, dodging between trees, and roll onto the summit knob at 5,252 feet. Stunted Douglas-fir limit the view from this small clearing, but Casey Peak in the Elkhorns and Mount Baldy in the southern end of the Belts rise above the valley to the southeast. Don't be tempted onto the "trail" that drops off the southeast flank of the mountain—it's an extremely steep (!!) erosion gully filled with head-sized boulders for a half-mile or more. Better to turn around and retrace your tracks to the cul-de-sac at mile 7.6. Try not to skid (dismount and walk if necessary), and yield to any uphill riders or hikers.

Scratchgravel Singletrack

Location: 6 miles north of Helena on the west end of the Helena Valley, in the Scratchgravel Hills.

Distance: 2.5-mile loop within the Scratchgravels.

Time: 15 to 20 minutes.

Tread: 0.8 mile on doubletrack; 1.7 miles on singletrack.

Aerobic level: Moderate, with one short but strenuous climb.

Technical difficulty: Mostly 3, with some sections of -4.

Hazards: Loose, sandy tread; prickly pear cacti just off-trail.

Highlights: This trail is one of the few locally that remains free of snow through much of the winter (except in heavy snow years; that's why they make skis). It also serves as a race course each spring for local mountain bikers. There's a lot of variety in its short length, with twisty, technical sections; flat-out runs with banked turns; and one hard climb to keep riders honest. Combine this loop with Rides 28 and 30 to put some singletrack spice into a tour of the Scratchgravels.

Land status: Bureau of Land Management and private property. Portions of this ride traverse private holdings, some of which may be posted against trespass. Please heed all posted property boundaries. Future access is uncertain.

Maps: Helena National Forest; USGS Scratchgravel Hills.

Access: Pedal out to the Scratchgravel Hills using either Head or Echo lanes (see Rides 28 and 30). To drive to the starting point, refer to the directions in Ride 30 for the Echo Lane Trailhead. The map on page shows additional routes from Echo Lane to the Head Lane junction and start of this ride.

The ride:

0.0   From Head Lane junction pedal north on rocky doubletrack as it climbs into the trees.
0.2   A doubletrack goes left; stay right on sandy doubletrack as it dips and climbs northeast.
0.4   Ride through a rocky, deeply eroded section that marks the beginning of more strenuous climbing. Stay to the

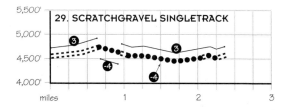

right where the track frays into several tracks going left and keep climbing. The route narrows and erosion gullies cut across the tread.

0.6   Watch for a cairn and colored flagging in the trees on the right just before a more difficult rocky section. Turn right at the cairn onto a narrow singletrack that contours into the trees. It dips and curves through sandy patches and over rocks, gradually dropping elevation.

0.8   Drop left to where an old dirtbike track joins in from the left. Bank right and enjoy smoother (faster) tread.

0.9   Lean right and downhill onto doubletrack. Keep your brakes ready—it's loose and rocky.

1.1   Watch for a banked singletrack turn cutting hard left (sometimes marked by yellow tape in a tree). If you pass an overturned blue car on the right, you've gone too far downhill on the doubletrack. The singletrack sweeps east and rolls through several shallow washes, dodging ponderosas and small boulders.

1.3   Swing hard right onto another old dirtbike trail and beeline west through those same shallow washes again. Back in the 1950s, when roads went over every little hill instead of cutting through them, they called these dips and rises "thank-you-ma'ams."

1.5   After climbing out of the last gully, slow again for a rock step going down, then cut 'er loose for a big banked turn right and a fast stretch through the trees.

1.7   Cross another wash, then a fading doubletrack.

1.8   Glance both ways as you zip across Head Lane—we're still up in the hills, but sometimes so are other bikers, horseback riders, pick-up trucks with dogs in back . . . . From here the trail climbs moderately, then more strenuously. Traction is good on this northeast side of the low ridge ahead.

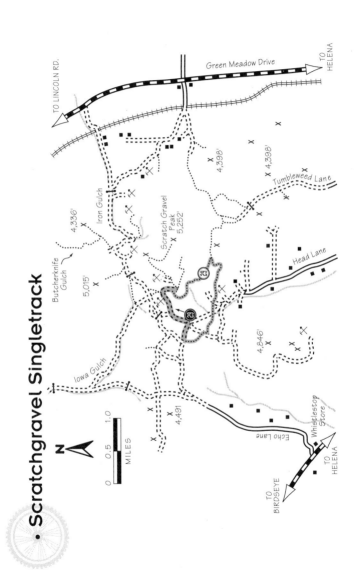

Scratchgravel Singletrack

TO LINCOLN RD.

Green Meadow Drive

TO HELENA

Iron Gulch

Butcherknife Gulch

4,336'

5,015'

Scratch Gravel Peak 5,252'

4,398'

4,398'

Tumbleweed Lane

Head Lane

Iowa Gulch

4,846'

4,491'

N

0   0.5   1.0

MILES

Echo Lane

Whistlestop Store

TO BIRDSEYE

TO HELENA

2.0 Push hard up a short but steep pitch through old diggings and onto the grassy ridge above Echo Lane to the west.

2.1 Turn right (uphill) onto well-defined doubletrack.

2.2 Just before the grade eases (near a knob capped by a handful of ponderosas on the right), watch for a faint, thin singletrack going left into the grass and sagebrush. The first 0.1 mile is rocky, but the runout beyond is smooth. Stay on the trail—cacti are abundant and well hidden in this area.

2.4 Drop onto the Echo-Head link road and turn right (uphill).

2.5 Pedal up to Head Lane junction to complete the loop. Now do it again, faster!

Echo Lane to Iron Gulch Loop

Location: 6 miles north of Helena on the west end of the Helena Valley, in the Scratchgravel Hills.

Distance: 18-mile loop.

Time: 1.5 to 2 hours.

Tread: 12.2 miles on paved road; 2.1 miles on gravel road; 3.7 miles on doubletrack.

Aerobic level: Easy to moderate, with a few strenuous but short climbs.

Technical difficulty: 1 on paved roads; 2 on gravel roads; 2+ to -4 on doubletrack.

Hazards: Watch for traffic on all roads. Stay on established roads and trails; these soils erode easily and prickly pear cacti are abundant. Expect flat tires if you wander off-trail. Ride in control and be alert for sand traps, ruts, slippery sidehills, and off-camber turns. In summer, carry extra water.

Highlights: Scant precipitation and sandy soils in the Scratchgravels mean dry trails and a longer riding season, even through winter in some years. There's also plenty of beginner and intermediate terrain, and a surprising (some say confusing) number of side trails. Watch for deer and a variety of birds.

Land status: Bureau of Land Management and private property. Portions of this ride traverse private holdings, some of which may be posted against trespass. Please heed all posted property boundaries. Future access is uncertain.

Maps: Helena National Forest; USGS Helena, Scratchgravel Hills.

Access: To do the loop described here, ride from town. Those who want a shorter ride entirely within the Scratchgravels can drive to the Echo Lane BLM access by following the ride description to mile 6.4. Park in the lot by the Birdseye Whistle Stop Store and pedal up Echo Lane. See Rides 28 and 29 for information on other routes in the Scratchgravels that enable you to loop back to Echo Lane.

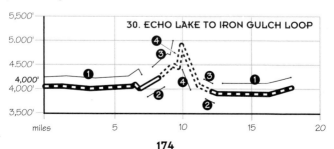

The ride:

0.0 From the Civic Center at the corner of Benton and Neill, pedal one block north then turn west on Hauser Boulevard.

1.3 Turn right on Joslyn Street and coast downhill.

1.5 Cross Euclid Avenue (U.S. Highway 12) at a traffic light. Continue north on Joslyn two blocks, then lean left to stay on the main paved road where Joslyn goes straight and becomes gravel. You're now on Country Club Road.

2.2 Spring Meadow Lake State Park on the left (swimming, fishing, boating, picnic shelters, restrooms, fee area).

2.5 Archie Bray Foundation for the Ceramic Arts on left.

2.8 Head Lane (gravel) goes right; stay on pavement, heading northwest.

3.5 Y junction; turn right onto Birdseye Road and pedal north between Fort Harrison's National Guard facilities.

4.1 Railroad crossing. The road swings left (northwest) for a long, gradual climb.

5.8 Follow the road right and over a second railroad crossing. Climb past two farmhouses and up and over a low hill.

6.4 Birdseye Whistle Stop Country Store and gas station. Pedal another 70 yards and turn right (north) onto the first gravel road—Echo Lane. A Bureau of Land Management sign and map are sometimes posted here. Echo Lane climbs a little steeply at first, through open sagebrush and grass at the foot of the Scratchgravel Hills.

7.9 Echo Lane continues, swinging right (northeast) toward the ridge at the head of Head Lane. Instead, veer left onto a sandy, deeply rutted doubletrack climbing north into a scattering of small ponderosa pines.

• Echo Lane to Iron Gulch Loop

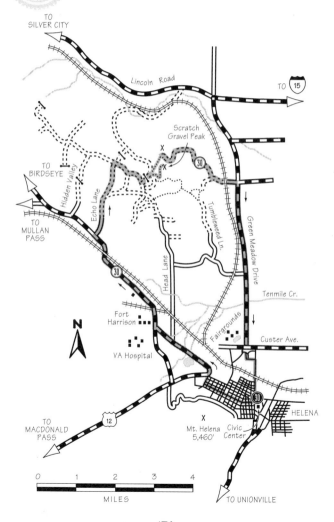

8.2 Make a 90-degree right turn at this crossroads and pedal east, climbing moderately on loose, gravelly doubletrack.

8.5 A doubletrack goes left to a nice view looking north, but don't be tempted to bomb down the hill beyond—it dead-ends at private property. Stay on the main track going east.

8.6 Faint doubletrack goes right; stay straight.

8.7 Grassy crossroads; stay straight on main track.

8.8 Doubletrack goes right to a short hillclimb; stay straight on main track.

8.9 Doubletrack goes hard right (0.2 mile to the link road between Echo and Head lanes). Instead, lean left into a soft, sandy corner. Resume moderate climbing on slightly smoother tread.

9.1 The main track angles toward a fenceline and comes to a three-way junction at a wire gate. Right leads to Head Lane and Rides 28 and 29. Instead, pass through the gate (please leave it as you found it), and take your pick of the two doubletracks ahead. The left track drops quickly only to climb again, and the right track contours on the level. They rejoin in 0.1 mile.

9.3 Roll up to another multi-choice junction. A hard right climbs 0.2 mile to join the Head Lane route toward Scratchgravel Peak (see Ride 28). The middle track is a shortcut to the route described below (it's an easier climb and saves about 0.1 mile), but we're going left and downhill.

9.4 Watch for an old cabin foundation—boards rotting on the ground—on the right. Go another 50 yards and slow for a hidden, off-camber turn to the right and uphill. If you ride out of the trees and into grasslands, you've gone too far downhill on the main Iowa Gulch Track (which dead-ends at a private gate in about 1.5 miles). The faint track rolls over a low hump of ground,

Echo Lane to Iron Gulch Loop—detail map

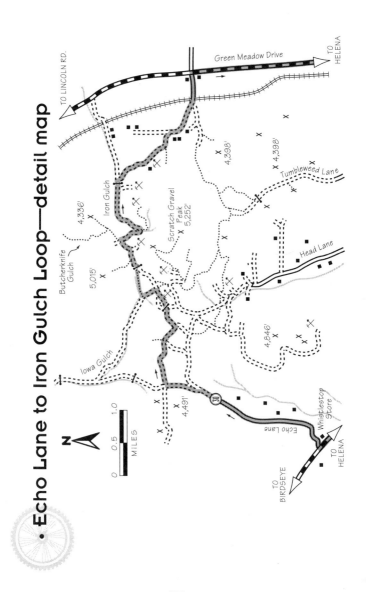

TO LINCOLN RD.

Green Meadow Drive

TO HELENA

Iron Gulch

Butcherknife Gulch

4,336'

5,015' X

Scratch Gravel Peak 5,252' X

4,398'

4,398' X

Tumbleweed Lane

Head Lane

Iowa Gulch

4,491' X

4,846' X

Echo Lane

Whistlestop Store

TO BIRDSEYE

TO HELENA

N

MILES

0   0.5   1.0

then drops to the sandy ravine bottom. Turn right up the ravine and enjoy some shade.

9.6 Gear down for a tough patch of rocks—a solid 4.

9.7 Grunt up a short but steep pitch out of the ravine bottom. Then lean left on the doubletrack that comes in from the right (from mile 9.3 above).

9.8 Cross through a gate in a barbed wire fence—please close the gate behind you. The tread grows rockier ahead.

9.9 A doubletrack goes left to climb the bald knob to the north, but it's too loose and steep to ride. Stay right on the main route and continue climbing, more strenuously now.

10.0 A doubletrack goes right 300 yards to old mine diggings; stay straight and climb onto the Scratchgravel Divide, with limited views east to the Big Belt Mountains. Ease down the loose, rocky jeep track going east.

10.1 A doubletrack goes left (dropping madly to a low saddle, with rough tracks splitting from there; one goes up the inviting but impossible hill to the northeast, and one runs down the gully to the north). Instead, lean right and continue down the rock-strewn road as it winds south and east.

10.2 Pass beneath a white-stained rock outcrop; look for hawks, prairie falcons, and other birds of prey.

10.3 Swing into a big left turn that falls away into a bowling alley of small boulders. (A vague singletrack splits right up a dark ravine at the apex of this turn. It leads to sandy doubletracks on the east flank of the main Scratchgravel Peaks—worth exploring, but watch for prickly pear.) The main route descends through rocks, ruts, and loose gravel—nasty stuff for the paint job on your bottom bracket.

10.5 A gravel road goes right and uphill (only to dead-end in about 0.3 mile at a bench and old mine, but the valley views are nice). Drop straight here.

10.7 Pass a shack on the right, then ride through a gate (please close it behind you).

10.8 The doubletrack forks; go hard right and roll south.

10.9 Another fork; go left and drop past old mine ruins.

11.0 Climb moderately for 0.1 mile to rejoin the track that went straight at mile 10.9.

11.2 Bounce down to a sandy wash (ignore the doubletrack going right), and climb quickly back up the other side.

11.5 Slow for a rocky, loose section, then rip down a smooth, fast run.

11.6 Join a dirt road and fenceline going south. Several drives lead to houses half hidden in the trees to the right; stay on the main road.

11.8 Doubletrack goes straight; veer left on the road.

12.1 At the Y junction go left 50 yards to a BLM map board and parking area. Rumble over the railroad crossing and drop down to . . .

12.2 Green Meadow Drive. Turn right onto pavement and watch for traffic as you roll back into town.

16.4 Traffic light and junction with Custer Avenue. Go straight at the green light and turn left onto Wedgewood Lane, which snakes east through the Sunhaven subdivision.

16.8 Turn right onto Fairway.

17.0 Turn left on Meadow Drive, then immediately right onto the wide asphalt walking path that parallels North Benton Avenue.

17.3 Cross three sets of railroad tracks. Continue uphill on an easy grade past the Benton Avenue Cemetery on the right and Carroll College on the left.

17.9 Traffic light at the corner of Benton and Euclid (US 12). Go straight south two blocks to close the loop.

18.0 Hauser and Benton. Find your way home from here.

Minnehaha–Bear Gulch Loop

Location: 10 miles west of Helena on the Continental Divide south of MacDonald Pass.

Distance: 16.5-mile loop.

Time: 2 to 4 hours.

Tread: 2 miles on gravel road; 6.8 miles on dirt road; 5.1 miles on doubletrack; 2.6 miles on singletrack.

Aerobic level: Strenuous, long, steep climbs alternating with moderate to easy downhill runs.

Technical difficulty: Mostly -3, but spots of -4 to 5. A handful of level-5 singletrack switchbacks complicate the end of the loop.

Hazards: Watch for traffic on Rimini and Minnehaha roads. Stay off the divide ridge sections of trail if storms or lightning threaten. Please close all gates and avoid spooking cattle; respect all private property. Ride in control, especially in rocky

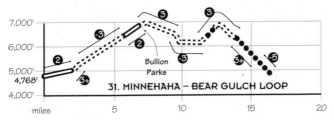

sections and switchbacks on the last 2.4 miles of singletrack. Do not attempt this loop if Tenmile Creek is too high to ford. Carry a rain or wind jacket, snacks, and extra water.

Highlights: A hill climber's delight, this loop is a double divide ride in miniature, with a screaming fun singletrack downhill to cap it off. Elk and deer are common along the divide ridge, and hilltop meadows offer outstanding views.

Land status: Helena National Forest and private property. Portions of this ride traverse private holdings, some of which may be posted against trespass. Please heed all posted property boundaries. Future access is uncertain.

Maps: Helena National Forest; USGS Three Brothers, MacDonald Pass, Black Mountain.

Access: From Helena drive 10 miles west on U.S. Highway 12. Turn left on Rimini Road (County Road 695) and drive 3.6 miles south to the Tenmile Picnic Area on the left. Park in one of two pullouts at the picnic area. The ride begins by pedaling south on Rimini Road, but the loop ends back at the picnic area, just across Tenmile Creek on the left side of the road. Before you start, check out the creek's water level: if the water is too high to ford (most likely in early spring), the loop described here cannot be completed.

The ride:

0.0   Pedal south from Tenmile Picnic Area on Rimini Road. Watch for traffic.
0.4   Pass Moose Creek Campground on the right; stay on main road.
2.0   A sign on the left by a parking pullout marks the Minnehaha Creek Road (Forest Road 527) on the right,

pointing to Bullion Parks at 5.5 miles. Turn right onto FR 527 and pedal across Tenmile Creek on a narrow bridge with white side rails.

2.1   The road forks; go left and begin a steep, rough climb. This is the rockiest and most strenuous section on the Minnehaha Road. Forest on both sides shades the road.

2.3   The grade eases to a moderate pitch and the road rambles upward along a narrow strip of private land.

3.6   Gear down for a more strenuous climb.

4.2   The grade eases somewhat.

4.5   A spur road goes right; stay straight on FR 527.

4.6   Grunt up another long strenuous section.

4.9   Grade eases slightly, then resumes climbing.

5.1   The road switchbacks right and the grade eases into the heavy-breathing end of moderate.

5.3   Switchback left. A doubletrack splits right at the apex; stay left on FR 527. The grade gets easier as the road traverses open slope.

5.8   Follow the road right into an open forest of lodgepole pine and grouse whortleberry. Enjoy almost level pedaling on fairly smooth tread as the road winds south and west.

6.0   Doubletrack goes left; stay on FR 527.

7.1   Pedal up to the crossroads and clearing at Bullion Parks atop the Continental Divide. FR 527 continues west and downhill. Instead, turn right onto rutted, mildly rocky doubletrack and climb north into a broad meadow along the divide.

7.2   A doubletrack goes left; stay right.

7.4   The doubletrack forks; go right. Soon wooden posts line the way. Please stay on the track here; the posts mark private property.

7.5   The grade levels off then rolls downhill in a mildly rocky, curvy run through open forest. Look for dia-

•Minnehahah–Bear Gulch Loop

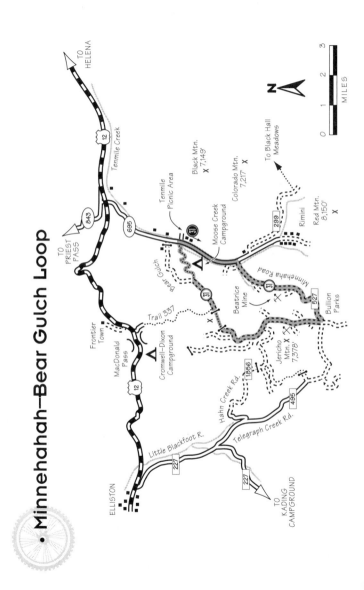

mond-shaped orange metal blazes posted on trees to mark the way.

7.8 A vague doubletrack goes right; stay straight on the main route.

7.9 The track breaks into a meadow and forks. The right-hand (and most obvious) fork rises to a high spot in the meadow with splendid views east to Black and Colorado mountains and south to Red Mountain. But go left at the forks instead, wrapping around the west edge of the meadow. The doubletrack drops quickly through a rocky and deeply rutted section in the trees.

8.2 Doubletrack goes left; stay straight.

8.3 Pass an old mine digging and another doubletrack on the left. Lean right and pedal through a short boggy spot.

8.5 Welcome to downtown Beatrice, once a bustling mining camp. The doubletrack hooks right and downhill, dodging tailing piles and stout mine buildings. Old cabin sites dot the surrounding woods.

8.6 Drop to a crossroads of sorts; the remains of a cabin mark the northeast corner. Go straight through the intersection, continuing a bouncy downhill run.

8.7 Slow for a boggy section—the muck here never fully dries out, and it can be shin deep in early summer. Skirt it by going uphill, walking through the trees if necessary, to avoid losing a shoe in the swamp. It's only 50 to 70 yards.

8.9 At the forks, go left, ignoring orange blazes leading right. These two tracks rejoin in about 70 yards, but the right one dips and climbs. You might as well stay on the easy left-hand track, which picks up the orange blazes again.

9.1 Dance downhill and abruptly out of the trees into a pug-ugly clearcut. This is private property, so it may not do any good to complain to the Forest Service about this logging-by-grenade style of timber management. The doubletrack becomes dozer track—a mix of unearthed boulders, shattered tree trunks, and mounds of raw dirt. Pick your way through the debris, aiming straight north, for about 0.1 mile. A national forest property sign shows where the doubletrack re-enters undamaged forest ahead.

9.4 Disregard a sign that reads "Road closed ahead—no turn around." A doubletrack cranks right here, up to a golden meadow, but stay on the main doubletrack going straight (northwest) and downhill.

9.6 Stop at a fenceline and let yourself through the gate. A sign indicates the route ahead is closed to motor vehicles, snowmobiles excepted. Close the gate behind you and drop left on a rough, rocky skidder track (a - 4) through an old clearcut.

9.7 Drop onto a graded dirt logging road. Ignore the orange blaze on the tree ahead (with an arrow pointing left), and turn right. Enjoy a long downhill run on fairly smooth tread as the road meanders north and east through brushy clearcuts and an occasional stand of trees.

10.4 The road swings right, then left, with trees on either side.

10.5 Drop into another cut-over area where the road forks. Bank right and uphill at the sign for Forest Road 1865-G1. A small, gray Continental Divide Trail sign, barely visible against the tree bark, also marks the way. Tall grass breaks this road into doubletrack as it climbs briefly, then levels off.

10.8 Slow for a rutted, rocky section.

11.2 The track swings east and south, then veers northeast again on a gradual downhill slant.

11.4 As the grade levels, watch for a Continental Divide Trail sign (on the left) that points right. A sign for FR 1864 marks the way. There's not much of a trail at first, just a wide, grassy corridor climbing east among scattered trees. Follow the cow pies and hoof holes as the corridor wanders left then right onto more obvious tread. The climb is on the moderate end of strenuous.

11.7 The cows seem to favor one side of this old doubletrack. The resultant trail banks left here and begins a more strenuous climb, hugging the shade at the meadow's edge.

12.0 The grade eases briefly. Follow the cow path as it stays to the right where the long meadow meets the forest.

12.1 The cow path veers right with the trees. Instead, go left on doubletrack that climbs hard toward a hill in midmeadow. A post halfway up the steep climb marks the divide trail.

12.3 The climb tops out on a grassy summit with another trail marker post and 360-degree views. Roll east and downhill on doubletrack into a narrow band of trees. Watch for gopher holes along the way.

12.5 Another cow path breaks right; stay left and dodge a downed tree. Then break into another meadow and begin climbing the next moderate to strenuous hill.

12.7 A trail crosses the doubletrack; stay straight.

12.8 Top of the hill. Pedal northeast, enjoying views north to MacDonald Pass and beyond.

12.9 Another trail marker post points left for the Continental Divide Trail, but there's no evident path through the tall grass. Instead, stay straight on the doubletrack, which drops and curves northeast.

13.1 Bounce down and into the trees, slowing for a rough rocky spot.

13.3 Roll into another linear ridgetop meadow, where the track alternates between double- and singletrack.

13.5 Lean left and into the trees on rough doubletrack. Grab the brakes for a steep, twisting drop with some -4 rocky and rutted sections.

13.7 Run through a small meadow, past an old corral on the right, then back into the trees on sinfully smooth tread.

14.0 A faint doubletrack goes right; stay straight.

14.1 Just when you think you've found doubletrack nirvana, steer right at a "trail" sign and tree-blaze onto singletrack. (The doubletrack soon dives down Bear Gulch toward the Rimini Road but dead-ends on private property.) The singletrack starts out smooth, contouring to the right.

14.2 Slow for a rocky, steeper stretch.

14.3 Lean into a left turn and onto smoother tread as the trail swings back and forth through shady lodgepole pine forest. Let 'er run, but scan ahead for pockets of rocky tread and possible downfall.

14.7 Bank for a right turn and drop a few gears if you like fast singletrack runs.

15.0 The trail ahead runs fairly smooth and sinuous for 0.5 mile. Wipe that grin off your face.

15.3 Traverse an open, south-facing slope where the trail is hidden under clumps of arrowleaf balsamroot.

15.5 Screech to a near halt for a sharp, loose switchback right (a 5+, but doable). Or walk your bike around the turn and enjoy views east to Black and Colorado mountains. Roll south on a long, gradual contour.

15.8 Crank through a sharp switchback left (-5).

15.9 Bounce down a 4+ rocky patch.

16.0 Follow the trail through a broad right turn and drop through dense forest.

16.1 Switchback hard left (5).

16.2 Switchback even harder right (5+).

16.3 Switchback left around rocks (5+) and into a wheel-tripping boulder garden (also 5+). Only the lucky survive. All others dab or crash.

16.4 Drop through tall grass onto doubletrack going right and left. Go straight across and dive through red osier dogwood and chest-high grass on singletrack that lands on the bank above Tenmile Creek. Look across to the Rimini Road and your vehicle at the picnic area parking lot. Wade or cross Tenmile Creek on logs or rocks, then bound up the other bank. Or just play in the water until all that trail dust (and wet cow pie) is knocked off.

16.5 Back at Tenmile Picnic Area.

Little Blackfoot Meadows Loop

Location: 25 miles southwest of Helena, along the headwaters of the Little Blackfoot River south of Elliston and U.S. Highway 12.

Distance: 14.8-mile loop; optional 8.8-mile up-and-back ride.

Time: 2 to 4 hours.

Tread: 2.4 miles on gravel road; 1.3 miles on doubletrack; 11.1 miles on singletrack.

Aerobic level: Mostly moderate, with a 1.8-mile strenuous climb at the halfway point. The loop ride described here rates as strenuous overall, while the up-and-back ride to Little Blackfoot Meadows is moderate.

Technical difficulty: 2 on gravel roads; 2+ to -3 on doubletrack; sections of -4 to 5 on singletrack.

Hazards: Watch for traffic on Forest Road 227 and on the first 1.1 miles of Trail 329. Roots and rocks are dangerously slick when wet. Grizzly bears have been reported sporadically in this area; make noise when riding through dense brush or near the creek. This is also a popular hunting area—wear an orange vest or avoid this area during hunting season. Always watch the weather: storms develop quickly on this side of the Continental Divide.

Highlights: The 4.4-mile ride into Little Blackfoot Meadows is a fun test piece for beginning and intermediate riders. The loop ride through Larabee Gulch offers a tougher challenge for more advanced riders. Either way, the scenery is wild and spectacular, with a good chance of seeing deer, elk, moose, and other wildlife. Side trails explore the ridges rimming the upper meadows.

Land status: Helena National Forest.

Maps: Helena National Forest; USGS Bison Mountain.

Access: From Helena drive about 20 miles west on U.S. Highway 12, over MacDonald Pass. Turn left (south) on the paved Little Blackfoot Road (Forest Road 227), 1 mile east of Elliston.

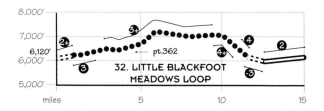

Drive south 2.6 miles (the road becomes gravel) and veer right to stay on FR 227 where Telegraph Creek Road (FR 495) goes left. FR 227 soon twists down to a bridge over the Little Blackfoot River, then swings south and west about 10 miles to Kading Cabin and Campground. (Watch for a washed-out bridge marking the mouth of Larabee Gulch—the ride's exit leg—about 8 miles from the Telegraph Creek Road fork.) Drive past the campground 0.5 mile to the parking lot and trailhead. Total distance from Helena to the trailhead is about 33 miles, half on gravel; allow at least 50 minutes of driving time.

The ride:

0.0 Trail 329 is well marked and begins as a four-wheel-drive road, a continuation of the access road. Large puddles are common, especially in early summer or any time after rain. Gear down for two moderate climbs and a few mild rocky sections (2+).

1.1 A short downhill leads to the original trailhead and the end of the "road." (Actually the road bends west here, listed on old maps as Trail 356; it runs onto private land in about 2.5 miles.) Pedal south on Trail 329, a wide dirt track at first. The tread soon turns rocky and root infested; gear down for two loose uphills.

1.4 The trail forks; go left and downhill to a footbridge over the Little Blackfoot River. From here the trail runs wide and almost easy through marshy lowlands. Numerous roots across the tread make for herky-jerky pedaling (and slick footing when wet).

2.5 Climb hard up the east bank and away from the river, jamming over more tree roots (-4).

3.5 Bounce downhill to cross the Little Blackfoot again, this

• Little Blackfoot Meadows Loop

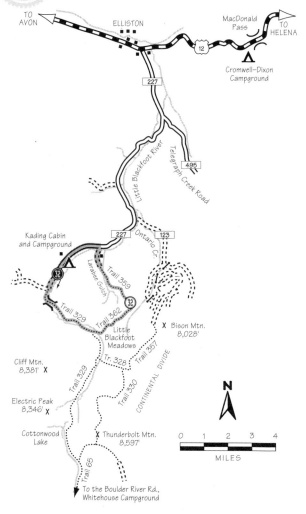

TO AVON

ELLISTON

MacDonald Pass

TO HELENA

12

Cromwell–Dixon Campground

227

Little Blackfoot River

Telegraph Creek Road

495

Kading Cabin and Campground

227

Ontario Cr.

123

32

Trail 359

Laravee Gulch

32

Trail 329

Trail 362

Little Blackfoot Meadows

X Bison Mtn. 8,028'

Cliff Mtn. 8,381' X

Tr. 328

Trail 357

Trail 329

Trail 330

CONTINENTAL DIVIDE

Electric Peak 8,346' X

Cottonwood Lake

X Thunderbolt Mtn. 8,597'

Trail 65

To the Boulder River Rd., Whitehouse Campground

N

0 1 2 3 4

MILES

time on a lone log. Then follow the recently reconstructed trail southeast along the west bank of the river.

4.4   At the junction with Monarch Creek Trail 362 it's time to choose between two main route options. Probably the most popular choice is to continue up Trail 329 to the right for 0.2 mile to Little Blackfoot Meadows. Campsites dot this subalpine basin (at 6,600 feet), and many bikers rest and eat lunch here before turning around and retracing their tracks back to the Kading trailhead.

    Strong, skilled riders with good route-finding skills can complete the loop outlined below by veering east onto Trail 362, signed for Monarch Creek. The trail winds along the north edge of the basin with many side trails running downhill on the right to horse camps; stay left on the main trail.

5.1   Begin climbing in earnest but pace yourself for the long, strenuous grade ahead. Anticipate steep surges, switchbacks, and loose tread. Near the top, rocks and roots give the climb a 4+ rating. The Forest Service plans to repair sections of this eroded trail beginning in summer 1997.

6.9   The grade eases into a high plateau at about 7,200 feet. Continue northeast through stands of stunted pines and alpine clearings with occasional views of 8,028-foot Bison Mountain to the east.

7.7   Grab the brakes as the trail aims downhill and into a rock garden (mostly 4).

8.1   Bounce out of the worst section of rocks into downfall (big trees can block the trail for years unless a trail crew spends an afternoon bucking firewood). Pedal gradually downhill another 0.1 mile.

8.2   Turn left (north) onto Larabee Gulch Trail 359. (If you miss this turn, the Monarch Creek Trail dives into a steep set of switchbacks with fat water bars; turn back.) Notice the blazes cut into trees—they'll come in handy later. Trail 359 climbs moderately back onto the plateau among weather-blasted trees.

9.6 The trail breaks into a high meadow and dwindles to a faint trace through tall grass. The grass hides chuckholes and large rocks, making it difficult to watch for blazes while picking your way through underbrush. Aim northwest and stay on the indistinct shoulder ridge that drops gradually into the head of Larabee Gulch.

10.1 The trail grows more defined again and soon falls into a set of six switchbacks. Narrow, loose, rocky tread and tight turns give this section a 4+ rating.

11.1 The grade eases and runs on smoother tread—but watch for washed-out sections.

11.7 Hang on for a steep drop to Larabee Creek. Splash across the creek and bomb downhill along the west bank.

12.2 Bump onto the old Larabee access road—a decent doubletrack that skirts a cabin.

12.4 Dip down to a washed-out bridge and the Little Blackfoot River. Rock hop across and turn left on FR 227 for the moderate grunt uphill to Kading. Watch for traffic.

14.3 Ride past the Kading Cabin and Campground.

14.8 Roll up to the trailhead and your vehicle.

MacDonald Pass–
Priest Pass Loop

Location: 15 miles west of Helena on U.S. Highway 12, atop the Continental Divide.

Distance: 18.5-mile loop.

Time: 2.5 to 3.5 hours.

Tread: 7 miles on pavement; 6.5 miles on gravel road; 3.3 on doubletrack; 1.7 miles on singletrack.

Aerobic level: 8.2 miles of fairly strenuous climbing (up to MacDonald Pass and along the divide). The remainder is moderate.

Technical difficulty: 1 on pavement; 2 to 3+ on double- and singletrack, with short sections of 4+ due to extremely rocky tread.

Hazards: Watch for traffic on US 12 and Priest Pass Road. Be prepared for strong winds and possible storms on the divide. Several rocky, technical sections can produce nasty falls.

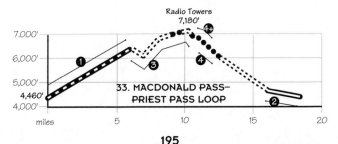

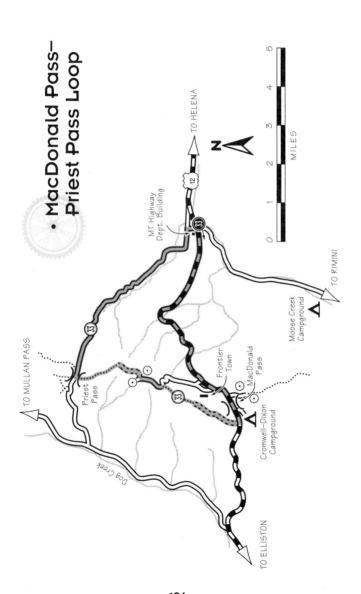

MacDonald Pass—
Priest Pass Loop

TO MULLAN PASS

33

Priest Pass

Dog Creek

33

MT Highway
Dept. Building

33

TO HELENA

12

N

Frontier
Town

MacDonald Pass

Cromwell-Dixon
Campground

Moose Creek
Campground

TO RIMINI

TO ELLISTON

MILES

0 1 2 3 4 5

Highlights: Good views from a challenging, seldom-used trail with a screaming descent on Priest Pass Road. There's a good chance of seeing deer and other wildlife.

Land status: Helena National Forest; private. Portions of this ride traverse private holdings, some of which may be posted against trespass. Please heed all posted property boundaries. Future access is uncertain.

Maps: Helena National Forest; USGS MacDonald Pass.

Access: From Helena, drive about 10 miles west on US 12. Just before the highway begins climbing toward MacDonald Pass, watch for a sign for Rimini on the left. Turn right here, onto a gravel road, and park on the roadside near the Highway Department's metal sheds.

To avoid biking up MacDonald Pass, leave one vehicle here and ferry the bikes on another vehicle west on US 12 to Forest Road 1894 at mile 7.0 in the ride description below.

The ride:

0.0 Pedal west and uphill on U.S. Highway 12 to MacDonald Pass. This is a 6.2-mile climb at a steady 8 percent grade. Plan on 1 hour to the top if you hump it. Traffic can be heavy at times; strong headwinds are likely, especially in the afternoon.

6.2 Top of 6,320-foot MacDonald Pass. Coast down the west side of the pass on US 12, enjoying a brief break from climbing.

7.0 Watch for a doubletrack heading into the grass on the right (north) shoulder. Turn in here and pedal north toward a small stand of trees. If the wind hasn't knocked it down, a sign marks this as Forest Road

1894. (For the car shuttle, park here next to the doubletrack, well off US 12. Leave room for vehicles to pass on the doubletrack.)

7.3   Fenceline and gate; please close gate behind you. Aim north and follow the doubletrack into the large meadow. Watch for cow pies in the tread and please don't spook the cattle.

7.9   Another fence and gate. The track climbs hard toward the divide ridge.

8.1   Pass a microwave relay station.

8.2   Top of the divide. Follow the doubletrack as it crosses to the east side of the ridge, with good views of the Helena Valley. The track roller-coasters along the divide, bearing north.

9.0   Hang on for a drop onto the east slope of the divide (watch for gopher holes). The track slices into the trees and drops east again, reverting to wide singletrack.

9.9   Climb through a clearing and several funky (but easy) switchbacks to join a gravel road, Forest Road 1802. Veer left and pedal north to the second set of microwave and radio towers.

10.3   The radio towers mark the highpoint of this ride at 7,180 feet. The main access road hooks right. Instead, turn left onto a rocky doubletrack at a signpost. Pedal north about 70 yards and watch for two trail signs on the right. One of these is a Continental Divide (CD) Trail marker. Bank right onto faint doubletrack that contours east and north.

10.4   The doubletrack enters forest and drops quickly.

10.6   The grade flattens out, but the tread disappears under a carpet of softball-sized rocks. Keep your wheels rolling and your weight on top of the bike—this short stretch is rideable, about a 4+. Stay on the main doubletrack, ignoring apparent side trails.

10.8 Enter an elongated meadow; stay on the left (western) edge of the clearing. The track devolves to singletrack.

11.0 Watch for CD Trail signs on the lone tree on the left edge of the meadow. Follow the singletrack leading northwest into the trees. From here the trail drops steadily, beelining north through a forest of spindly lodgepole pine.

11.5 Another small meadow. Where's the trail? Look right, at about 2 o'clock, for a CD Trail sign. Bounce down through the trees again, ignoring game trails that cross the main route.

12.0 Another meadow. Descend left on the trail, dodging boulders and root steps (rate it a 4). It's easy to focus close to your front wheel, but keep an eye ahead so you can find a rideable line.

12.2 Hang on for a steep, loose drop (3+).

12.5 The trail runs out into a clearing on Priest Pass and joins Priest Pass Road (FR 335). Ready to give your brake fingers a rest? Try the jeep tracks going north from the road for some challenging hillclimbs. When you're ready to finish the loop ride, pedal east on Priest Pass Road. It loses elevation gradually at first, then begins a series of hard turns and seriously out-of-control drops. CAUTION: Anticipate sharp turns, off-camber curves, and loose gravel. Control your speed. Also watch for traffic on this narrow road. It eventually eases and cuts through a neighborhood of cabins and ranchettes.

18.3 Bank right on the main road (straight ahead goes to US 12).

18.5 The Highway Department sheds and your car.

34

Great Divide Ski Area

Location: 24 miles northwest of Helena on the Continental Divide above the old mining town of Marysville.

Distance: Nine rides, varying in length from 2 to 6 miles.

Time: 15 minutes going up the lift; 10 minutes to 1 hour cruising back down the mountain.

Tread: Mostly doubletrack and jeep road, with some sections of singletrack.

Aerobic level: Easy for the handful of all-downhill rides (ain't lift-assisted biking grand?). Some rides include uphill sections ranging from moderate to fairly strenuous.

Technical difficulty: 2+ to 5. Most rides contain a variety of terrain and tread conditions. Rocks, loose gravel, and soft spots are common. Switchbacks on singletrack rides are rideable, from 3 to 4+.

Hazards: Ride in control at all times. Watch for other trail users, including hikers. Yield to faster cyclists on downhills. The chairlifts are equipped with seat belts for people unaccustomed to swinging over treetops. Expect winds and cooler temperatures along the ridge and at higher elevations; dress accordingly.

Highlights: Great Divide offers Helena's only lift-assisted mountain biking . . . an easy way to get your bike to the top of a 7,200-foot mountain. The views are spectacular and the riding options nearly unlimited. Roads and trails radiate off

Mount Belmont onto adjacent national forest and Bureau of Land Management lands. Hone your downhill skills, then enjoy lunch or dinner at the Continental Club in the base lodge.

Land status: Private; Helena National Forest; Bureau of Land Management.

Maps: Ask for a copy of the Great Divide ski trails map at the lodge. Bike routes are not marked, but the map shows the major drainages and ridges. Helena National Forest; USGS Canyon Creek, Greenhorn Mountain.

Access: From Helena drive 8 miles north on Green Meadow Drive, Montana Avenue, or Interstate 15 to Lincoln Road (County Road 279). Turn left and drive northwest 7 to 10 miles to gravel Marysville Road (CR 216), on the left about 0.5 mile west of Al's Silver City Bar. Drive another 6.3 miles west to Marysville and bear left on the main road (a sign points toward Ophir Creek). The road winds steeply uphill; bear right where Ophir Creek Road splits left (0.9 mile above Marysville) and drive to the ski area parking lot and lodge at road's end, a total of 24 miles from Helena.

The rides:

Readers, squeeze your brakes . . . we're gonna detour briefly from the standard format here. The folks at Great Divide opened their hill to mountain bikers several years ago; they even hosted a race or two. Then in 1996 they modified the Mount Belmont chairlift to carry bikes and flagged nine or ten routes down the mountain.

That first season the lift ran from 11 a.m. till 5 p.m. on most Sundays, from late June through September. A single ride ticket was $5, and an all-day pass cost $10. As of this writing,

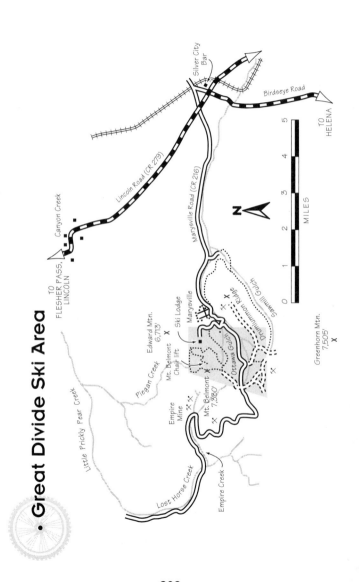

Great Divide Ski Area

TO
FLESHER PASS,
LINCOLN

Canyon Creek

Lincoln Road (CR 279)

Silver City
Bar

Birdseye Road

TO
HELENA

Marysville Road (CR 216)

N

MILES

0 1 2 3 4 5

Little Prickly Pear Creek

Piegan Creek

Edward Mtn.
6,713'
X

Mt. Belmont Chair lift
X

Ski Lodge

Marysville

Drumlummon Ridge

Sawmill Gulch

Empire Mine
X X

Mt. Belmont
7,380'
X

Ottawa Gulch

X

Greenhorn Mtn.
7,505'
X

Lost Horse Creek

Empire Creek

202

expect the same set-up for upcoming seasons, which usually begin by late June. Call (406) 449-3746 for an update.

You don't have to be a diehard downhiller to enjoy dangling your feet on the ride up and jangling your adrenals on the ride down. There are several all-road options (with some doubletrack) for beginners, while intermediate and advanced riders will enjoy getting lost on a surprising array of jeep tracks, trails, and livestock or game runs. If enough people support this service, the number of routes will surely expand, whether flagged by Great Divide crews or simply blazed with fat tire tracks in the tall grass.

One caution: even the easiest rides here require off-road bike-handling skills. Expect steep drops, loose gravel, and sudden changes in tread conditions. Beginners can handle the easier routes, but ride cautiously (don't give in to the temptation to dive like a kamikaze back to the bottom). Experienced mountain bikers know that uphills may be painful, but downhills are where the real injuries occur. Ride in control at all times. Volunteer bike patrollers are sometimes on duty to help anyone that gets lost or hurt, but all riders are responsible for their own safety.

You also need to be prepared for the rugged terrain and mountain weather. Bring extra clothes, including a wind or rain jacket, full-fingered gloves, and a hat that will fit under your helmet. Don't forget a water bottle, and bring a trunkful of tools, including a spare inner tube. Tighten all nuts and bolts, check your tire pressure, and make sure your brakes are ready and able before you leave the parking lot.

Then find out how much vertical you can do in a day!

Rogers Pass to Flesher Pass

Location: 45 miles north of Helena, between Montana Highway 200 and County Road 279 (Lincoln Road).

Distance: 13.5 miles.

Time: 3 to 6 hours.

Tread: 3 miles on doubletrack; 10.5 miles on singletrack.

Aerobic level: Strenuous! There are numerous long, steep climbs at high elevation. Only strong, skilled riders should attempt this ride.

Technical difficulty: Mostly 3+, but with frequent and sustained sections of 4 to 5 due to loose shale, rocks, steep grades, switchbacks, narrow tread, and strong, buffeting winds.

Hazards: Much of this route traverses open, wind-blasted ridges above 7,000 feet. Expect high winds, cold temperatures, and sudden changes in weather. Do not attempt this route if

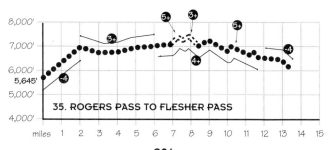

35. ROGERS PASS TO FLESHER PASS

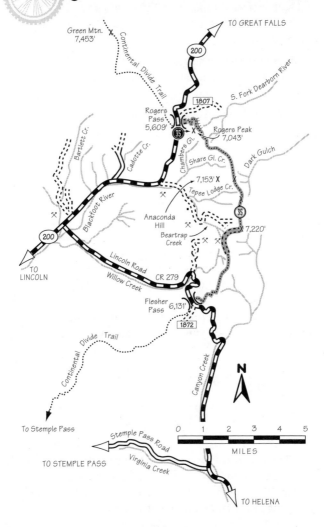

• Rogers Pass to Flesher Pass

TO GREAT FALLS

200

S. Fork Dearborn River

1807

Green Mtn.
7,453'

Continental Divide Trail

Rogers
Pass
5,609'

35

Rogers Peak
7,043'

Bartlett Cr.

Cadotte Cr.

Chambers Gl.

Share Gl. Cr.

Dark Gulch

7,153' X

Tepee Lodge Cr.

35

Blackfoot River

Anaconda
Hill

7,220'

Beartrap
Creek

200

Lincoln Road

CR 279

TO
LINCOLN

Willow Creek

Flesher
Pass 6,131'

1872

Continental Divide Trail

Canyon Creek

N

To Stemple Pass

0   1   2   3   4   5

Stemple Pass Road

MILES

TO STEMPLE PASS

Virginia Creek

TO HELENA

storms or high winds are likely. Allow plenty of daylight, and carry extra clothing, rain gear, waterproof matches, and ample food and water. Pack tools and a spare inner tube just in case. Also be alert for bears near the trail, particularly during spring and midsummer.

Highlights: Spectacular, rugged alpine scenery; 360-degree vistas of surrounding mountains, including the Rocky Mountain Front; wild, remote, and challenging terrain.

Land status: Helena National Forest.

Maps: Helena National Forest; USGS Rogers Pass, Wilborn.

Access: This ride is best done with a vehicle shuttle. Plan to leave one car at Flesher Pass so you can drive back to the trailhead on Rogers Pass.

From Helena drive north 8 miles on Interstate 15, Montana Avenue, or Green Meadow Drive to Lincoln Road (County Road 279). Turn left and drive west about 30 miles to Flesher Pass. Leave one vehicle here in the pullout on the left side of the road. Then drive down the north side of the pass 8.5 miles to MT 200. Turn right and drive 7.5 miles east to Rogers Pass. About 0.4 mile before the pass, a Forest Service sign marks the site of the coldest recorded temperature in the contiguous United States. Drive about 0.3 mile east and turn right onto a steep doubletrack marked by a blue Continental Divide Trail sign. Park well off the doubletrack, either in a flat meadow just above the highway, or 100 yards uphill at the actual trailhead.

The ride:

0.0 The trail threads between a few trees and immediately begins climbing strenuously. The tread was freshly cut in 1995–1996 and is still loose and rough. Be ready to lunge over fat and frequent water bars.

0.1 The grade levels off briefly. Follow the trail left and across a stout plank bridge. Then resume the steep grind uphill on an open slope.

0.2 Splash through a small stream.

0.3 Switchback right and sit on that rear tire to keep traction on the steep, loose grade ahead.

0.4 Cross two more small streams, then switchback left.

0.6 Switchback right. The trail finds a bit more soil in places, improving traction. But steep sections prevail.

0.8 Switchback left and begin a rolling contour east to more open slopes.

1.2 Gear down for a long, strenuous stretch on poker-chip sized shale. It's deep and loose, making the grade feel even steeper than it is.

1.5 Switchback right. Enjoy the views opening up north, east, and west. At this point the wind usually makes itself felt; it'll be stronger on the ridge above.

1.8 Swing right (west) across an open slope below rock walls, then swing left into a large grassy meadow.

2.0 Top of the initial climb and the point of no return. If the first 2 miles were daunting, turn around now after admiring the views, and enjoy the descent back to your vehicle.

Ready for the run to Flesher? Look south to see several miles of the trail ahead cutting across the rocky spine of the divide. Cairns mark the way at strategic points.

2.1 Drop quickly to a notch in the ridge and contour south.

2.7 Begin a strenuous climb on loose shale.

2.9 The trail levels off along the wind-blasted ridge, then drops west.

3.0 Hit the brakes for two sharp switchbacks, right then left, both loose and shaley.

3.1 Drop to a shallow saddle with great views of the banded cliffs on the eastern face of the divide. The trail becomes faint as it crosses a littering of shale. Just stay on the ridgetop until you pick it up again. Then enjoy an easy downhill run on the west flank.

3.5 Cruise into a stand of trees and a respite from the wind.

3.6 Climb hard left and out of the trees, then ease into a contour across open slopes.

4.3 Lean right and climb a long, strenuous grade.

4.7 The trail levels off briefly.

4.8 Resume the steep climb, snaking through broad turns on rocky tread.

4.9 Head back into the trees, where the grade soon eases.

5.3 Switchback left and drop down a rock-strewn, loose pitch.

5.8 Drop into granny gear for another steep climb followed by a rolling, rocky stretch punctuated by short climbs.

6.3 Bust a move up a truly steep (!), loose pitch to a small knob. This is perhaps the first unrideable section, harbinger of things to come. Rumor is that the Forest Service may re-route the trail here and at mile 6.8, adding switchbacks to ease the grade. Don't hold your breath—at least not at this altitude.

6.8 Everybody dismount and push the bikes up a sustained 30-degree slope buried in shale. A barely visible doubletrack leads southwest to a cairn near the top.

7.0 Walk onto the summit, shale crunching underfoot like broken dishes. If the wind was blowing 40 mph at mile 2, expect 60 mph here. The doubletrack curves left on shale bedrock, then favors the lee side of a second knob going south. Watch for abrupt ledges and walk your bike as needed. From the second knob the trail drops southeast to a small dip in the ridge.

7.3 Follow faint doubletrack up another steep, unrideable slope. Ignore the game trail that cuts across the scree slope to the right—footing there is too unstable.

7.5 A wooden post marks the top of a broad summit knob, and the trail vanishes. Make a 90-degree right turn, just above a stand of gnarled pines, and pedal 50 yards southwest. Here the doubletrack becomes more defined and drops steeply on loose rocks across the top of an old clearcut.

8.2 Zip down through a small meadow where a wooden post marks the trail. Lean left onto an old logging road that skirts more of the clearcut.

8.5 Turn right and climb strenuously on what looks like an endless grade, with the snag-filled clearcut on the left. The road swings left and wraps around the hillside, climbing hard to the south.

9.0 The climb tops out. Turn left onto singletrack where trail signs point the way and drop through a grassy clearing.

9.1 Drop over a small shale step.

9.2 Drop and twist over another small step.

9.4 Brake for a steep drop that curves right, then roll on fairly level ground among trees just left of the ridge's rocky spine.

9.6 Drop again, leaning right to join doubletrack on an old logging road.

9.7 The doubletrack curves right, but a Continental Divide Trail sign points left to the singletrack chopped into the hillside.

10.0 Climb out of the trees, curving right and onto doubletrack.

10.2 The track forks, with a CD Trail marker in the middle. Go right and roll downhill.

10.4 The doubletrack goes straight at a CD Trail marker. Lean left onto rough singletrack dropping fast. Watch for rocky sections and frequent dips and bumps in the tread.

10.7 Fallen rock litters the trail—5+ or unrideable. Ride the next 70 yards of trail, but walk the second stretch of talus. The third boulder garden soon thereafter is easier, a 4+.

11.0 Slow for a sharp switchback left and drop to a smooth tread in the pines.

11.2 Gear down for a strenuous climb up short but steep switchbacks on loose tread.

11.4 The grade levels and rolls by a cairn.

11.6 Climb right and roll around a small rock outcrop.

11.8 Bank around another outcrop and drop onto a fast contour north.

12.2 Slow for a sharp switchback left, then pull the ripcord as the trail dives into the trees on pine duff tread.

12.4 The trail rolls through a wide corridor in the pines, then angles left to contour around the slope.

12.8 Hang on for the final descent toward Flesher Pass. It tends to be rocky and loose in spots.

12.9 Pause at a rock outcrop that overlooks the highway and the drainage south toward Canyon Creek. Lean right and continue descending.

13.1 Swing around one last sharp switchback left and bounce downhill on scattered fist-sized rocks.

13.3 Slow for a rockier than usual patch (a -4).

13.5 Break out of the forest above the road at Flesher Pass. The trail is built up on 10-inch square timbers and drops into the roadside ditch in two steps. The shoulder is made of deep, loose cinders. Watch for traffic.

See Appendix A for information on continuing the ride along the Continental Divide Trail south from Flesher Pass to Stemple Pass.

Vigilante National Recreation Trail 247

Location: 25 miles northeast of Helena, about 6 miles east of York, in the Big Belt Mountains.

Distance: 2.4 miles one way, with several route options from the far end.

Time: 50 minutes to 1.5 hours going up; 20 to 45 minutes coming down.

Tread: 2.4 miles of singletrack.

Aerobic level: Strenuous, with several quasi-moderate intervals.

Technical difficulty: 3+ with frequent spots of 4 to -5.

Hazards: Narrow tread; occasional downfall. Yield to other trail users.

Highlights: Strong intermediate and advanced riders will enjoy this trail's smorgasbord of challenges, from roots, rocks, and water bars to narrow, trenched tread and quad-popping climbs. Wildflowers are abundant in early summer, and deer and elk frequent the forests and clearings along the upper ridge. The route is described here as a short up-and-back ride, but other route options allow for an 8-mile up-and-back extension, or a long loop ride out Magpie Gulch.

Land status: Helena National Forest.

Maps: Helena National Forest; USGS Hogback Mountain, Snedaker Basin.

Access: From Montana Avenue on the north end of Helena drive east on Custer Avenue, passing over Interstate 15 and continuing past the airport. This road becomes County Road 280 as it leaves town. At 1.4 miles from Montana Avenue, bear left at the sign for York (Canyon Ferry Road goes straight). Continue northeast another 16.7 miles, past Lakeside Marina, across York Bridge over the Missouri, and up a winding canyon to the crossroads at York (the York Bar is on the left). Go straight at the crossroads, staying on the paved road. The asphalt ends in 3.3 miles and the road is now labeled Forest Road 4137; continue another 3.4 miles to road's end. Turn right and cross the bridge over Trout Creek to enter Vigilante Campground. The trail begins between two campsites on the northeast end of the campground loop road. Total distance from Helena to the trailhead is 25 miles; figure at least 45 minutes of driving time.

The ride:

0.0 From the campsite, climb hard up a steep singletrack. Two fat water bars pose the greatest challenge to riding this first pitch clean. The trail dips in and out of an old ditch, then veers left onto a well-defined trail (a right turn here drops you back to the campground).

Optional ride to Hanging Valley Overlook

36. VIGILANTE RECREATION TRAIL 247

Vigilante National Recreation Trail 247

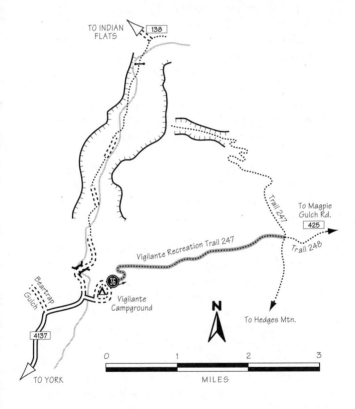

TO INDIAN FLATS

138

To Magpie Gulch Rd.

425

Trail 247

Vigilante Recreation Trail 247

Trail 248

Beartrap Gulch

4137

36

Vigilante Campground

To Hedges Mtn.

N

TO YORK

0   1   2   3

MILES

0.2 The grade eases briefly. The trail loops through a gully and climbs across an open, south-facing slope.

0.3 Again the grade eases; two spur trails go left to overlooks above the lower end of Trout Creek Canyon. Resume climbing on the main trail as it bends east.

0.5 Catch your breath as the trail levels off briefly then continues climbing.

0.7 Dip through a small side gully.

0.9 Another quick dip through a side gully. From here the trail rolls through dense underbrush, alternating between moderate and strenuous grades.

1.4 Cruise into an open forest of lodgepole pine and enjoy a level section of trail.

1.6 The trail cuts back into the undergrowth and dives sharply into a gully, banking left. Then it climbs strenuously across a loose, sandy slope with a few root steps thrown in for fun.

1.7 As the trail bends right it begins a tough, 0.2-mile root-infested stretch. This climb should be moderate, but it feels strenuous because the roots break up any pedaling rhythm. At least it's rideable—nothing too big to grind up and over.

2.0 Just as the roots start to thin out the climb turns truly strenuous. A scattering of gravel and fist-sized rocks keeps things interesting.

2.1 The climb eases but the tread goes from bad to worse. The trail crosses a 30-foot patch of clinkers—flakes of rock scattered below the mother stone above. Strong, skilled riders may be able to power over the bumps and wheel traps, but this section rates a solid 5. Don't be surprised if you walk it. Free of the rocks, the trail climbs easily through the shade of lodgepole pine.

2.4 A trail junction in a small grassy clearing marks the top of the ridge between Trout Creek and Magpie Gulch.

An unofficial dirtbike trail wings off to the right and uphill along the ridge toward Hedges Mountain. Straight ahead a sign points right and downhill to Magpie Gulch Trail 248 and Magpie Gulch Road (Forest Road 425). A third option (for determined bikers with too much time on their hands) is to bank left and into the trees to continue on Trail 247. This trail climbs hard onto a spur ridge, wraps into a small gully, and climbs again around a larger spur ridge. Then it switchbacks madly down a north-facing slope into Hanging Valley, finally turning west beneath tall cliffs. After about 4 miles, the trail stair-steps down to a viewpoint high above Trout Creek Canyon. Retrace your tracks to return to the trailhead.

Trout Creek Canyon

Location: 25 miles northeast of Helena at the north end of the Big Belt Mountains.

Distance: 3 miles one way.

Time: 30 minutes to 1 hour going up; 20 to 45 minutes coming down.

Tread: 1 mile on narrow gravel "road"; 0.2 mile on doubletrack; 1.8 miles on singletrack.

Aerobic level: Moderate, with a few short but mildly strenuous pitches.

• Trout Creek Canyon
• Hogback Mountain

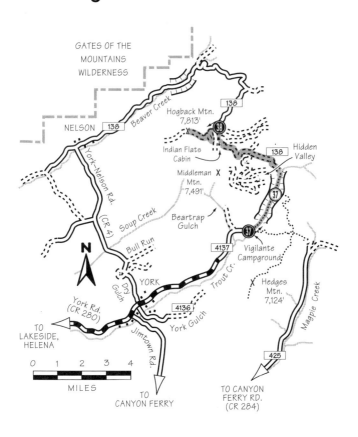

GATES OF THE
MOUNTAINS
WILDERNESS

Beaver Creek

NELSON 138

138

Hogback Mtn.
7,813'
X 38

Indian Flats
Cabin

138 Hidden
Valley

York-Nelson Rd.

Middleman X
Mtn.
7,491'

37

(CR 4)

Soup Creek

Beartrap
Gulch

37

Bull Run

4137 Vigilante
Campground

N

Trout Cr.

X Hedges
Mtn.
7,124'

Dry Gulch

YORK

4136

York Rd.
(CR 280)

York Gulch

Magpie Creek

TO
LAKESIDE,
HELENA

Jimtown Rd.

0 1 2 3 4

MILES

TO
CANYON FERRY

TO CANYON
FERRY RD.
(CR 284)

425

Technical difficulty: The first mile is mostly smooth with one or two rocky patches—2+, suitable for beginners. The remaining 2 miles mix abrupt climbs with rock gardens and loose gravelly tread, ranging from 3 to 5 in difficulty.

Hazards: Rough, rocky sections can trap wheels or bounce bikes off the trail. Ride in control, especially where the trail skirts steep dropoffs. Watch for other trail users. Spring floods often alter the trail, particularly where it crosses the creekbed (which is bone dry during most summers above the crossing at mile 0.5).

Highlights: Spectacular limestone cliffs tower 1,000 feet above the narrow creekbed and trail, sheltering a variety of plants and birds. Deer, black bear, and cougar are occasionally seen. The trail itself follows what's left of the old roadbed that washed away in a major flood some years back. In places it offers a fine technical challenge, with longer intervals of easier riding. Except for a handful of abrupt climbs, the grade is moderate (though scree, rock gardens, and other obstacles may compel riders to gear down into tractor mode).

Land status: Helena National Forest.

Maps: Helena National Forest; USGS Hogback Mountain.

Access: From Montana Avenue in north Helena drive east on Custer Avenue, crossing over Interstate 15 and continuing past the airport. This road becomes County Road 280 as it leaves town. 1.4 miles from Montana Ave., bear left at the sign for York

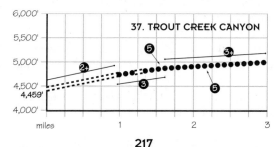

217

• Trout Creek Canyon

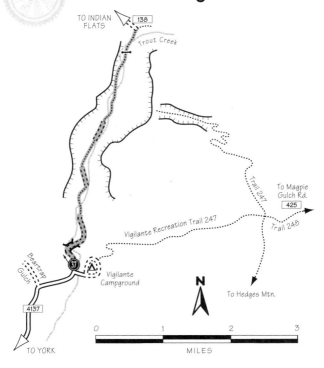

TO INDIAN FLATS

138

Trout Creek

To Magpie Gulch Rd.

425

Trail 247

Trail 248

Vigilante Recreation Trail 247

Beartrap Gulch

37

Vigilante Campground

4137

N

To Hedges Mtn.

TO YORK

| 0 | 1 | 2 | 3 |

MILES

(Canyon Ferry Road goes straight). Continue northeast another 16.7 miles, past Lakeside Marina, across York Bridge over the Missouri, and up a winding canyon to the crossroads at York (the York Bar is on the left). Go straight at the crossroads, staying on the paved road. The asphalt ends in 3.3 miles and the road becomes Forest Road 4137; continue another 3.4 miles to Vigilante Campground and the trailhead at road's end. Total distance from Helena to the trailhead is 25 miles; figure at least 45 minutes for driving time.

The ride:

0.0 From the parking lot pedal north onto Trail 270—the wide gravel track that climbs easily above Trout Creek. This "trail" follows the remnants of an old roadbed. In 1995 the Forest Service groomed the first 0.9 mile of trail to improve access, though it's not quite barrier-free (a standard wheelchair might not make it far). Please ride slowly on this stretch and yield to other trail users.

0.2 Cross a stout wooden bridge over Trout Creek and continue the gradual climb into the canyon.

0.5 Cross another bridge over Trout Creek. At the time of this writing the Forest Service was installing a plank bridge here. Until that's completed (or if spring runoff washes it away), a large log offers a way to walk across. Bounce up a mildly rocky section to rejoin the old roadbed going north.

0.8 Cross an old road bridge.

1.0 The road dwindles to doubletrack, then wide but rocky (3+ that looks worse than it rides) singletrack.

1.1 A faint trail goes left to the creekbed. Instead, lean right and uphill into the trees.

1.3 Drop left to a dry (usually) crossing of the creekbed, and continue on gravelly doubletrack that quickly reverts to singletrack on the old roadbed.

1.5 Begin climbing more moderately.

1.6 Veer left onto a tread of loose rock rubble. It climbs steeply for 20 yards; this section rates a -5 to 5+ depending on how many big rocks have fallen onto the trail and how churned up the rubble is from other cyclists and horse traffic. The trail tops out, then bumps back down to creek level.

1.7 Cross the creekbed and climb a steep pitch for 20 feet. Enjoy an all-too-short smooth section through forest on the right side of the creek. The trail breaks onto a remnant of the old roadbed again, then skirts beneath a smooth, overhanging cliff face.

2.0 Trout Creek washed away the trail here during spring 1996. Hug the rock wall on the right and drop into the creekbed for a rough crossing. The user-created trail jogs up the left bank, then wraps right around a clump of trees and bashes back across the creek. Depending on how broken down the banks are at these crossings, cyclists may have to dismount and walk.

2.2 Gear down for a sharp climb to a hippopotamus-sized bump capped with a bedrock step. Going up is a solid 5 (it's a -5 on the way back). Drop down the other side of this obstacle and run through the bushes that clog the trail.

2.3 Bounce in and out of the creekbed twice, ending up on the left-hand side. Ahead the cliffs close in on either side, reminiscent of the narrow sandstone canyons in southern Utah. The trail contours steeply up a loose, rocky slope, then drops back down to creek level. It swings across to the right side only to veer left and cross again, rolling through a shady stretch in the trees left of the creekbed.

2.8 Cross to the right-hand side and roll up to a barbed-wire fence. Please close the gate behind you. Cross again to the left bank and climb a strenuous but short pitch. Roll down the other side onto an almost level grade.

3.0 The trail breaks out of the trees into a small parking area with Forest Road 138 coming in from the left. This marks the turnaround point for the Trout Creek Canyon ride. Those who want to continue can pedal west up FR 138 to the Indian Flats cabin and Hogback Mountain (see Rides 38 and 39).

The return trip down Trout Creek Canyon tends to go faster than the trip up. Ride in control and expect some fat-tire rodeos on the way back.

38

Hogback Mountain

Location: 30 miles as the crow flies northeast of Helena at the north end of the Big Belt Mountains.

Distance: 2.6 miles one way.

Time: 20 to 50 minutes going up; 10 to 15 minutes coming down.

Tread: 2.6 miles on one-lane gravel road.

Aerobic level: Strenuous, with a surprising amount of near-moderate climbing.

Technical difficulty: 2+.

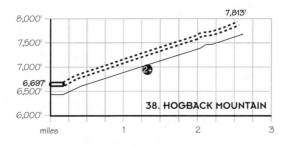

. Hogback Mountain

[also see map on page 216]

Hazards: Watch for traffic. Staff at the Forest Service tower on top have counted as many as fifty cars a day on this road—thirty cars a day is average on summer weekends. Also watch for sharp turns and loose gravel on the return trip downhill. Ride in control at all times. Do not attempt this ride if storms or lightning are likely; the open ridge offers no shelter.

Highlights: Absolutely spectacular 360-degree views from atop 7,813-foot Hogback Mountain. On a clear day, the views reach from the Anaconda-Pintlers in the southwest to the Highwoods in the northeast. With the Helena Valley and Canyon Ferry spread out below, and the Elkhorns, Gates of the Mountains Wilderness, and Big Belts folded all around, it's like looking down on one of those 3-D molded plastic relief maps. The fire lookout is staffed from July through September.

Land status: Helena National Forest.

Maps: Helena National Forest; USGS Hogback Mountain.

Access: From Montana Avenue on the north end of Helena drive east on Custer Avenue, crossing over Interstate 15 and passing the airport. This road becomes County Road 280 as it leaves town. About 1.4 miles from Montana Avenue, bear left at the sign for York (Canyon Ferry Road goes straight). Continue northeast another 16.7 miles past Lakeside Marina, across York Bridge over the Missouri, and up a winding canyon to the crossroads at York (the York Bar is on the left). Go left at the crossroads and drive 8.2 miles on the gravel York-Nelson Road (CR 4) to the outpost of Nelson ("Cribbage Capital of the World"). Turn right here onto Beaver Creek Road (Forest Road 138) and stay on this main road as it winds northwest through a limestone chasm, then switchbacks up to Indian Flats. This section is closed to motor vehicles from April 15 to June 1 for wildlife security.

About 14.7 miles from Nelson, the road tops out in a vast meadow at a junction with Forest Road 298—the route to Hogback Mountain. Park here, well off the road. The total distance from Helena is about 41 miles.

The ride:

0.0 Yes, the road ahead is open to motor vehicles, but it's more adventurous on a bike. Pedal south and slightly downhill on FR 298 toward the wooded base of Hogback Mountain.

0.2 FR 298-A1 goes left; bear right on FR 298. A sign warns of steep, narrow road ahead. The first pitch is on the steep end of moderate.

0.4 Switchback left and keep climbing.

0.9 The grade eases then switchbacks hard right. This turn is so sharp that motor vehicles have to go straight and make a little loop on the gravel pad at the apex of the turn.

1.1 The grade slants upward at a strenuous pitch. It soon swings left, then hooks south for the open ridge.

1.5 The grade eases briefly.

1.6 Swing right and gear down for another strenuous section.

1.8 Ease onto the ridgetop and start enjoying the views. Follow the road west toward a radio tower and building.

2.0 Gear down for another strenuous climb. Crosswinds here can add to the effort.

2.3 The road levels off as it passes the radio tower. Look ahead to see the final climb to the Forest Service fire lookout building.

2.5 Start the final climb. It can be done in the middle chainring if you've got any legs or lungs left at 7,800 feet.

2.6 Roll up to the fire lookout at 7,813 feet. Do this on a clear day and you can see a third of Montana simply by turning a full circle on your heels. Closer at hand, the rocks at your feet are suffused with fossilized shells and other marine life forms. The ridge road continues west a few tenths of a mile, dropping elevation slightly before ending high above Checkerboard Gulch. Retrace your tracks on the main road to get down Hogback Mountain.

Other popular options for Hogback Mountain include riding to the top and back from Trout Creek Canyon (see Rides 37 and 39), or driving to the top and riding downhill to York (east) or Nelson (west). For either of the two latter options, have somebody shuttle the car back downhill to meet you at the end of the ride. To reach York going east, reverse the ride outlined in Ride 39. To reach Nelson, retrace the route described above: ride back down FR 298 to FR 138 and bear left. The road runs north for nearly 5 miles and turns through a half-dozen switchbacks before swinging southwest along Beaver Creek. It's about 17.3 miles from the summit to Nelson. Allow 40 minutes to 1.5 hours for the mostly downhill run.

Indian Flats

Location: 30 miles northeast of Helena at the north end of the Big Belt Mountains.

Distance: 8.1 miles one way, with an optional 2.6-mile extension to the summit of Hogback Mountain.

Time: 1.5 to 2.5 hours going up; 40 minutes to 1 hour coming down.

Tread: 5.2 miles on narrow gravel road; 0.2 mile on doubletrack; 1.8 miles on singletrack.

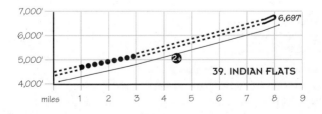

Aerobic level: Moderate, with a few short but mildly strenuous pitches.

Technical difficulty: Trout Creek Canyon starts off as a 2+ but then turns rocky, ranging from 3 to 5 in difficulty. The road ride to Indian Flats is mostly smooth; rate it a 2.

Hazards: Rough, rocky sections in Trout Creek Canyon can trap wheels or bounce bikes off the trail. Ride in control, especially where the trail skirts dropoffs. Watch for other trail users. Spring floods often alter the trail, particularly where it crosses the creekbed (bone dry during most summers above the crossing at mile 0.5). Watch for the rare vehicle on Forest Road 138 to Indian Flats. Ride in control on the return trip, braking early for sharp turns.

Highlights: Spectacular limestone cliffs in Trout Creek Canyon; beautiful meadows and open forest on the climb to Indian Flats. Look for deer, elk, black bears, and cougars. This route offers access to Hogback Mountain (see Ride 38) and Indian Flats cabin, which can be rented from the Forest Service (call ahead for reservations). For an extended stay, drive food, water, sleeping bags, and extra clothes up to Indian Flats cabin, then start the ride back in York. Spend the next day doing day rides from the cabin. On the third day drop down to Nelson and back to York via Beaver Creek Road (FR 138) and County Road 4.

Land status: Helena National Forest.

Maps: Helena National Forest; USGS Hogback Mountain.

Access: From Montana Avenue on the north end of Helena drive east on Custer Avenue, crossing over Interstate 15 and passing the airport. This road becomes County Road 280 as it leaves town. About 1.4 miles from Montana Avenue, bear left at the sign for York (Canyon Ferry Road goes straight). Continue northeast another 16.7 miles past Lakeside Marina, across

York Bridge over the Missouri, and up a winding canyon to the crossroads at York (the York Bar is on the left). Go straight at the crossroads, staying on the paved road. The asphalt ends in 3.3 miles; from here the road is labeled Forest Road 4137. Continue another 3.4 miles to Vigilante Campground and the trailhead at road's end. Total distance from Helena to the trailhead is 25 miles; figure at least 45 minutes of driving time.

The ride:

The first 3 miles of this route are described in greater detail in Ride 37.

0.0 From the parking lot pedal north onto Trail 270—the wide gravel track that climbs easily above Trout Creek. This "trail" follows the remnants of an old roadbed.

0.2 Cross a stout wooden bridge over Trout Creek and continue the gradual climb.

0.5 Cross another bridge over Trout Creek. Bounce up a mildly rocky section to rejoin the old roadbed going north.

0.8 Cross an old road bridge.

1.0 The road dwindles to doubletrack, then wide but rocky (3+) singletrack.

1.1 A faint trail goes left to the creekbed. Instead, lean right and uphill into the trees.

1.3 Drop left to a dry (usually) crossing of the creekbed, and continue on gravelly doubletrack that quickly reverts to singletrack on the old road bed.

1.5 Begin climbing more moderately.

1.6 Veer left onto loose rock rubble as the tread climbs a steep grade (-5 to 5+) for 20 yards. The trail tops out, then bumps back down to creek level.

• Indian Flats

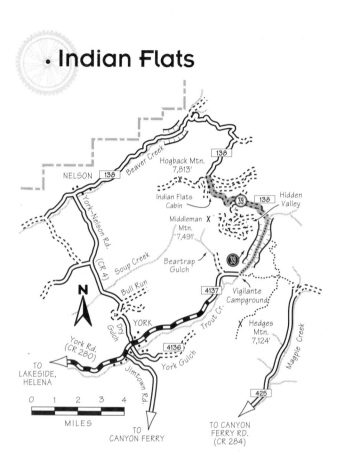

1.7 Cross the creekbed and climb a steep pitch for 20 feet.
Enjoy smooth tread through forest on the right side of
the creek. The trail breaks out in the open onto a remnant of the old roadbed again, then skirts beneath a
smooth, overhanging cliff.

2.0 Trout Creek washed away the trail here during spring 1996. Hug the rock wall on the right and drop into the creekbed for a rough crossing. The user-created trail jogs up the left bank, then wraps right around a clump of trees and bashes back across the creekbed.

2.2 Gear down for a sharp climb to a hippopotamus-sized bump capped with a bedrock step (rate it a 5). Drop down the other side and run through the bushes that clog the trail.

2.3 Bounce in and out of the creekbed twice, ending up on the left-hand side. Ahead the cliffs close in on either side. The trail contours steeply up a loose, rocky slope, then drops back down to creek level. It swings across to the right side only to veer left and cross again, rolling through a shady stretch in the trees left of the creek.

2.8 Cross to the right-hand side and roll up to a barbed-wire fence. Please close the gate behind you. Cross to the left bank and climb a strenuous but short pitch. Roll down the other side onto an almost level grade.

3.0 The trail breaks out of the trees into a small parking area with Forest Road 138 coming in from the left. This marks the turnaround point for the Trout Creek Canyon ride. To reach Indian Flats, pedal west up FR 138. A beautiful, linear meadow runs below the road on the left side, taking some of the strain out of this long, steadily moderate climb.

3.5 Switchback right.

3.8 Switchback left. Look left over the edge to glimpse odd limestone pillars and cliffs. According to the Helena National Forest map, some cartographer saw the shape of a barking dog in one of these rocks.

4.0 The road levels off.

4.2 FR 138-F1, an old logging spur, goes right. Bear left and enjoy a brief downhill run.

4.6 Resume moderate climbing.

5.0 Forest Road 4119 goes left and downhill into the meadow. This old logging spur offers 5 to 7 miles of scenic riding through deep forest and small limestone canyons, including Hidden Valley. A spur also climbs the east flank of 7,491-foot Middleman Mountain through clearcuts.

To continue on to Indian Flats, pedal uphill on FR 138.

5.2 Switchback left. FR 138-E1 goes uphill and right into Bowman Gulch at the apex of the turn. Stay on the main road.

6.1 Loop through a big switchback right. Then the road swings left and contours northwest.

6.4 FR 138-D1 goes right; stay straight on the main road.

6.7 Cross a cattleguard.

7.6 A sign marks the side road to Indian Flats Guard Station, a cabin that the Forest Service rents to the public. Another 10 yards up FR 138, Forest Road 4118 goes right (an enjoyable ramble along Grouse Ridge).

8.1 Roll into Indian Flats and a junction with Hogback Mountain Road (FR 298). You've got three options from here: 1. Enjoy lunch if you brought it with you, then zoom back down to Trout Creek Canyon and the trailhead. 2. Turn left onto FR 298 and grunt uphill 2.6 miles to the fire lookout atop Hogback Mountain (the views are stupendous—see Ride 38). Then zip back down to Trout Creek. 3. Continue north on FR 138 to drop into the Beaver Creek drainage, a 15-mile downhill run to Nelson. Then climb south on CR 4 about 8.2 dusty miles to York, turn left, and ride the final 6.7 miles up to Vigilante Campground and the trailhead. This last option adds up to a 40-mile loop, mostly on dirt and gravel roads.

Cave Gulch Loop

Location: 25 miles northeast of Helena on the east side of Canyon Ferry Lake.

Distance: 17.3-mile loop.

Time: 2 to 4 hours.

Tread: 1.2 miles on paved road; 6.8 miles on gravel road; 9.3 miles on ATV track.

Aerobic level: Strenuous.

Technical difficulty: 1 to 2 on roads; mostly -3 to 4 on Trail 243, with a spot or two of 5+ near the end of the trail.

Hazards: Watch for traffic on roads and ATV traffic on Trail 243. The descent through Cave Gulch is fast and fun; it tempts many riders to push their limits. But the track is also riddled with natural hazards, so ride in control at all times. Carry plenty of water to replenish your fluids after the hard initial climb.

Highlights: The Cave Gulch ATV trail offers bikers the most outrageous downhill run in the area: 4.4 miles of banked turns, whoop-de-doos, and gut-bottoming dips on fairly smooth tread. In places alder and maple form a tunnel over the trail, and the scenery—a bit blurry at speed—is spectacular. From start to finish, this loop is always entertaining. The ride up Magpie Gulch makes an easy, pastoral warm-up, and the ridge section of Trail 243 (after 0.5 mile of steep! uphill) offers a hint of what waits in Cave Gulch. Wrap it all up with a burger and beverage at O'Malley's for a great day in the hills.

Land status: Helena National Forest and private property. This trail is maintained by a local ATV trail users group, which has worked diligently to preserve access to and from Cave Gulch across several private parcels.

Maps: Helena National Forest; USGS Canyon Ferry.

Access: From downtown Helena drive east on 11th Avenue, which becomes U.S. Highway 12/287 as it crosses Interstate 15 and leaves town. Drive east about 11.5 miles on US 12/287 (through East Helena) and turn left at the flashing yellow light onto County Road 284. Drive another 11 miles north and east, crossing Canyon Ferry Dam and passing through the Bureau of Reclamation village at the north end of the lake. CR 284 (now Canyon Ferry Road) wraps around the east side of the lake here and heads south. About 0.3 mile past the turn for Chinaman Gulch Campground (on the right), turn left into a sprawling dirt parking lot at O'Malley's Bar and Restaurant (a total of about 23 miles from Helena). Park on the left.

The ride:

0.0   From O'Malley's turn left on paved Canyon Ferry Road (CR 284) and pedal south on a gradual climb.

0.7   Crest the hilltop and spin down into Magpie Gulch.

1.2   Magpie Bay Road goes right; lean left on the main road

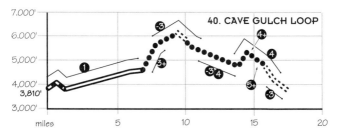

Cave Gulch Loop

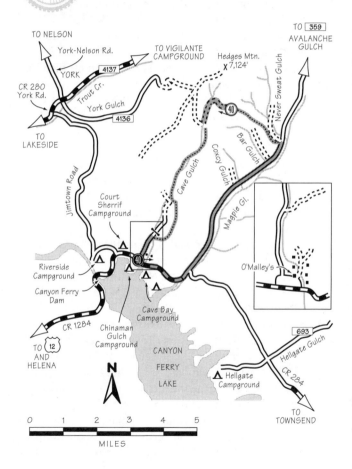

TO NELSON

York-Nelson Rd.

TO VIGILANTE
CAMPGROUND

Hedges Mtn.
X 7,124'

TO 359
AVALANCHE
GULCH

YORK

4137

CR 280
York Rd.

Trout Cr.

York Gulch

4136

40

Never Sweat Gulch

TO
LAKESIDE

Cave Gulch

Coxcy Gulch

Bar Gulch

Jimtown Road

Court
Sherrif
Campground

Magpie Gl.

O'Malley's

Riverside
Campground

40

Canyon Ferry
Dam

CR 1284

Chinaman
Gulch
Campground

Cave Bay
Campground

693

Hellgate Gulch

TO 12
AND
HELENA

CANYON
FERRY
LAKE

Hellgate
Campground

CR 284

TO
TOWNSEND

N

0   1   2   3   4   5

MILES

and bounce off pavement onto graded gravel road. Watch for traffic. Pedal east past ranchettes and summer homes.

2.0   The road forks. CR 284 bends right; instead, take the left-hand fork, Magpie Gulch Road (FR 425).

2.5   Cross a cattleguard. The road narrows and continues climbing at an easy grade.

4.6   Coxcy Gulch Road goes left; stay straight on FR 425.

6.0   Bar Gulch Road goes left—this was the old trailhead for the Cave Gulch Trail, but the Forest Service decided the old trail was hazardous and an erosion problem waiting to get worse. The new trailhead is in Never Sweat Gulch; stay straight on FR 425.

6.8   Turn left onto FR 425-C1, a doubletrack running up the meadowy bottom of Never Sweat Gulch. Pedal about 200 yards in from Magpie Road and look for an ATV track curving left to a trail sign at the edge of the meadow.

6.9   Drop into granny gear and crawl up the steep ATV track that cuts left across the base of the south flank of the gulch. Whoever named this Never Sweat never pushed a bike out of the gulch. Watch for erosion ruts and large rubber water bars across the trail.

7.0   Switchback right—by now most folks are walking. The steep (!) grade ahead is on the verge of being rideable . . . if you've got legs like Secretariat and lungs the size of Macy's parade balloons. At least it's shady.

7.2   The grade eases as the trail breaks into a grass and sagebrush clearing on the nose of a spur ridge.

7.3   Resume the strenuous climb straight up the fall line. Serious hammerheads can grind up this on-ramp to heaven; most folks walk it after attempting the lower third.

7.5 Gasp onto the ridgetop, pause to enjoy the views, then bank right at a trail sign. The trail levels off, allowing a coasting run through some gentle turns before climbing again.

7.8 Gear down for a strenuous (!) pitch, trending left to a low knob. The trail rolls northwest along the ridge, entering an open forest of ponderosa pine.

8.2 Grunt up another 100 yards at a strenuous pitch, then ease onto an almost moderate grade.

8.4 Climb again—it's not as steep or long as the last pitch. From here the trail undulates along the ridge at a moderate clip, meandering around trees and gradually gaining elevation.

9.0 Drop a gear or two for a slightly steeper section.

9.2 Clank into granny mode and stay on the right side of the track to climb hard along an erosion rut. Repeat after me: "We're almost to the top of the initial climb."

9.5 The trail bends left and enters a small grassy clearing. Roll down to a signed Y junction. The left track follows an old logging road. Instead, follow the trail sign pointing right and enjoy a gradual downhill through forest. CAUTION: The next 4.4 miles are too much fun. Banked turns, continuous whoop-de-doos, shallow puddles, and nonstop downhill may cause short-term memory loss ("Climb? What climb?") and big-stupid-grin syndrome. But seriously, ride in control and watch for unexpected dropoffs, sharp turns, big rocks, and branches across the trail.

9.8 Roll out into a revegetated clearcut and lean left at the next Y junction. The tread grows a bit rocky and drops quickly into the head of Cave Gulch. Small whoop-de-doos encourage aerobatics here.

10.1 Slow for a sharp turn left (or skid to a stop on the runaway bike ramp, dead ahead). Grab the brakes for a steep drop into a bowl-shaped meadow, trending left on banked turns.

10.3 The plunge eases to a smooth, fast runout.

10.6 The track banks right, crossing a small stream, and splits. Lean onto the left fork, following the signs for Cave Gulch Trail 243. The tread narrows slightly and grows ever more sinuous, swoopy, and full of surprises. No need for odometer readings here because the dips, twists, banked turns, and opportunities for air time are continuous . . . just hang on and enjoy.

11.8 Bounce across two short wooden bridges.

12.2 The trail continues its E-ticket descent. Alder and maple encroach upon the trail, forming tunnels on some stretches. Watch for slap-happy branches, some at nose height.

13.9 The track forks. The right branch goes to private property, so bank left, drop into a small gully, and spin into granny gear for an abrupt, strenuous climb (Oomph! Have you forgotten how to ride *up*hill?) up the bottom of a ravine. Stay left where another track goes right.

14.0 Steep!? Yup. Get off and walk as the trail scampers up the left side of the ravine.

14.1 The grade eases enough to let you pedal, then runs almost level.

14.3 Bank right and genuflect before you begin another strenuous climb through open forest.

14.4 Roll onto level trail in a grassy clearing, then drop south into another small gulch.

14.9 Slow for a rocky spot (4+ for difficulty), then roll beneath a rock outcrop and plunge down and right. Dance through another rocky spot (4), then run smooth through the trees.

15.1 Dip in and out of a small gully and resume a moderate climb to a grassy clearing on a low ridge. Bear right and climb strenuously as the trail stair-steps up a limestone hogback. Loose, rocky tread gives way to big bedrock steps—a 5+ near the top.

15.4 Top out on a rocky knob with excellent views southeast over Canyon Ferry Lake to the flank of the Elkhorn Mountains. Then play mountain goat and scramble along the hogback atop the ridge (mostly level 4 moves).

15.6 Put your rear over the rear wheel for a short but steep (!) and loose drop. The grade eases.

15.8 Bank right (the doubletrack goes straight) and fall into a steep (!), loose chute.

15.9 The grade eases and the track forks. The right-hand trail dives into the trees; instead, go left along the ridgetop.

16.1 Brake down another loose, gravelly pitch to a trail sign and a T junction with what looks almost like a dirt road. Turn left and follow the "road" through a gap in a wire fence (several ATV tracks go right and left here).

16.2 Drop sharply right to a tangle of ATV tracks in a small clearing. Follow an obvious track left and downhill.

16.3 Stay left at a Y junction.

16.4 Bounce onto a narrow gravel road and go left.

16.8 Pass the national forest boundary sign and roll by a scattering of homes (please stay on the main road).

17.3 Watch for traffic as the road dumps into the parking area around O'Malley's. Time to celebrate and knock the mud off your teeth with a cold beer or soda pop.

Some riders dislike the climb out of Never Sweat Gulch so much that they avoid it entirely by starting the ride in York. From the crossroads at the York Bar, pedal east up York Gulch Road (FR 4136) as it climbs—moderately at first, then more strenuously—about 6 miles before dropping to meet Cave Gulch Trail 243 at mile 10.6 as described above. From the end of the trail at O'Malley's, pedal back to York on Jimtown Road, which runs north from below Canyon Ferry Dam. To avoid biking Jimtown Road, leave a car at O'Malley's and shuttle back to York to begin the ride.

Appendix A

Other Helena Area Routes

If the 40 rides featured in this book just aren't enough, here are a couple of seasons' worth of roads and trails that bear exploring. The descriptions here are intentionally sketchy—based on either the author's perforated memory or secondhand rumors from suspect sources (i.e., friends who have spent way too many hours in oxygen debt).

Close to Town

Mount Helena Foothills Trail - A thin, rocky trail runs along the base of Mount Helena on the north side, below the Prairie Trail and above LeGrande Cannon Boulevard. Although the main east-west route is seeing more use now than in years past, it still feels like an old cow path meandering through the rocks and sage. Though the grade is easy, technical sections give this ride an overall 4+ rating. Access points: **(1)** From the corner of the chainlink fence around the water tank where the 1906 Trail leaves the Adams Street parking lot. Bank right and ride past a picnic table, then head downhill and left. This footpath crosses the Holter Street Access Trail, then runs up a shallow draw between the Quarry Trail and a low hogback; **(2)** From the corner of Holter Street and LeGrande Cannon Boulevard scramble up the singletrack that skirts the last house on Holter to the south. This trail drops through a small gully, then climbs southwest toward Mount Helena. Stay to the right and watch for a narrow trail diving back into the gully, to the right. If you miss this one, another trail just ahead also breaks west to join the Foothills Trail; **(3)** A steep, rocky (is it rideable?) trail climbs up from LeGrande just east of Grant Street to a four-way junction below the Quarry Trail; **(4)** From LeGrande, pedal uphill and south on O'Reilly Street, then right on Charlie Russell, left on Gary Cooper, and right on Mount Helena Drive. A signed trail leaves from the west end of Mount Helena Drive, dipping through a ravine, then climbing onto a broad, sloping bench below the cliffs on Mount Helena. Numerous trails branch out from here, including the Northside Access Trail, which contours up to the Foothills Trail in about 100 yards. The Northside trail continues west into trees and then switchbacks hard to join the Prairie Trail at Sunset Point. Easier trails also run west from below the Northside Trail, linking Mount Helena

City Park with the network of jeep tracks and trails coming off of Early Summer—Seven Sisters Ridge (see Rides 7 and 8).

Tucker Gulch - Several trails run south toward Skihi Peak from the upper end of Tucker Gulch, which is the east arm of Dry Gulch south of Davis Street in Helena (see Ride 18). Recent land deals between a private landowner, the city, and the Forest Service have clouded access issues, however, and these routes may be closed in the near future.

Cox Lake Cutoff - This isn't a ride so much as an important link between the Unionville Road and Dry Gulch. From Helena cyclists can reach the lower end by riding 3.6 miles south up the paved Unionville Road. Turn left onto gravel Springhill Road. To reach the upper end from town, pedal south up Davis Street, which becomes Dry Gulch (gravel) as it leaves town (see Ride 18). Turn right at mile 2.4 and climb hard 1 mile to Dry Gulch Estates and a view of private Cox Lake. Take the first road on the left immediately west of the lake. Look for an easy-to-miss singletrack going right off this private drive. The trail threads south between private yards on either side, then splits into doubletrack and begins a gentle downhill into a wooded draw. After about 0.4 mile the track turns to sandy, rutted road and enters a grassy opening. Continue downhill on graded, residential Springhill Road. Please stay on the main road (all side roads here are private driveways) and ride in control. The posted speed limit is 5 mph. About 1 mile from Cox Lake this route lands you on Unionville Road 0.1 mile downhill from Unionville.

Park Lake - This shallow lake and its adjacent campground are popular destinations for Helenans hoping to escape summer heat in the valley. From Helena drive south through Unionville over the Orofino–Lump Gulch Divide on CR 454 and FR 4000. After about 13 miles turn right onto Lump Gulch Road (FR 4009) and drive another 9 miles to Park Lake at road's end. Old logging and mining roads in the area offer several ride opportunities. Two of the best are: **(1)** Pedal back down FR 4009 to Chessman Reservoir, then ride around to the reservoir's southwest shore. A trail follows the aqueduct from Chessman over to the road above Rimini on a nearly level grade. The route is unmaintained, so expect downfall. **(2)** Lava Mountain ATV Trail 244 is a new route connecting Park Lake to Cataract Basin in Deer Lodge National Forest. This wide track runs about 8 miles to the head of Cataract Creek, where a network of old mining roads run south to the town of Basin or north to Cataract Meadows and 8,076-foot Old Baldy Mountain.

West End of the Scratchgravel Hills - The west end of the Scratchgravels sees less public use than the main hills off Head Lane. That's partly because there are no loop opportunities or public access west of Echo Lane. Follow the directions to Echo Lane given in Ride 30. At mile 8.2 in that description turn left instead of right and climb onto the low Scratchgravel divide. A rocky doubletrack rolls east among sage and prickly pear. Mining claims dot the BLM land and side roads branch right and left at regular intervals. After about 4 miles the track grows rougher and forks—left and hard uphill for a view from the backside of the Birdseye area, or right and downhill through old diggings to dead-end at a private fenceline above the head of Silver Creek. Landowners on Silver Creek, Hidden Valley, and other Birdseye-area roads have asked the public not to use their roads to enter or leave the Scratchgravels. Retrace your tracks to Echo Lane for the trip back to town.

Continental Divide

Telegraph Creek - The logging roads at the head of Telegraph Creek offer easy rides through dense lodgepole forest studded with the ruins of the Lily-Orphan Boy, Sure Thing, and Ontario mines. These can be reached as either **(1)** an extension of the Minnehaha Road loop (see Ride 31), or **(2)** by driving west from Helena on US 12 over MacDonald Pass to the Little Blackfoot Road (FR 227). Stay left where the road forks and drive about 2.5 miles up to the national forest boundary. In another 2 miles numerous spur roads begin to branch left and right. Or stay straight south on the main road to reach the historic Ontario mining district. **(3)** Another option here is to park at the turn for Hahn Creek Road (FR 1856), just under 2 miles from where Telegraph Creek Road forks off from the Little Blackfoot Road. Ride up Hahn Creek about 4 miles, then bank left on FR 1836 and follow signs for the Continental Divide Trail south down Jericho Creek to rejoin Telegraph Creek Road. Turn right and roll north to return to your car.

MacDonald Pass south - From Helena drive 15 miles west on US 12 to the top of 6,320-foot MacDonald Pass. Turn left onto a dirt road and drive south 1 mile to a parking lot on a bald knob by a radio tower. Trail 337, one of the less rideable sections of the Continental Divide Trail, dives off the knob and beelines south along the divide. It's 4.5 miles of rough-and-tumble trail (sometimes 5 to 5+ boulder gardens) with a few strenuous climbs to the Bear Gulch Trail (Ride 31); the trail junction is in a high meadow with splendid views.

MacDonald Pass Cross-Country Ski Trails - Beginning riders looking for short off-road rides away from the buzz of town will enjoy these ski trail loops. Drive 15 miles west on US 12 up to MacDonald Pass and park in the lot on the access road at Frontier Town. A wide trail drops into the trees just north of the fighting bear statue and joins four doubletrack loops that run north from Frontier Town along the east flank of the divide. The 2.8-mile Old Cabin Loop is the shortest and easiest, and the 6-mile Little Porcupine Loop is the longest and covers a wider variety of terrain. For more information on these trails, ask for the "MacDonald Pass X-C Ski Trails" brochure (Forest Service publication number R1-90-15), which has a rough map of the area. The brochure is available at both the district ranger's office and the Helena National Forest office in Helena.

Granite Butte - From Helena drive north and west on Lincoln Road (CR 279) about 28 miles. Turn left onto Stemple Pass Road (CR 601) and drive 9 miles west to 6,736-foot Stemple Pass atop the Continental Divide. Park in the lot on the north side of the road. There are two main options here: **(1)** Pedal south, following either FR 485 or the Continental Divide Trail, running parallel and just east of the road. Both routes climb for almost 3 miles and rejoin where the Granite Butte spur road branches east and south. Gear down for the steep, rocky climb as this jeep track wraps 1.7 miles around the south flank of the mountain to the lookout tower on the 7,600-foot summit. Return to your car by retracing your tracks; count on at least 1 hour for the round trip. **(2)** If you can arrange a shuttle, leave one vehicle at the Canyon Creek Store (about 21 miles from Helena on Lincoln Road). After climbing Granite Butte, return to FR 485 and turn left to ride south along the divide. In about 2 miles FR 484 dives off the east face of the Divide and swoops down Marsh Creek through aspen groves and shady fir forests. It's 9 or 10 miles down to Little Prickly Pear Road (CR 707), then another 6 miles east to Lincoln Road and the Canyon Creek Store. Plan on 2 to 3 hours for the 25-mile one-way ride.

Flesher Pass to Stemple Pass - This section of the Continental Divide Trail offers a longer but somewhat less strenuous ride than its cousin, Ride 35. It's best done with a vehicle shuttle. From Helena drive 28 miles north on Lincoln Road (CR 279), turn left, and drive 9 miles on CR 601 to Stemple Pass. Leave a car here in the lot on the north side of the road. Then drive the second vehicle back down to Lincoln Road and turn left, driving another 9 miles north to Flesher Pass. Park in the large pullout on the left side of the road. Ignore gated FR 1872 and start instead on the trail uphill, marked with a Continental Divide Trail sign. The trail climbs, then roller-coasters up and down along the divide for about 15 strenuous miles. Nearing Stemple Pass, the trail drops onto old logging roads and bends south to join CR 601. Depending on which logging roads you take, total trip distance is about 18 miles; set aside at least 3 hours.

Big Belts

Magpie-Avalanche Gulch Loop - Magpie Gulch Road (FR 425) climbs deep into the Big Belt Mountains on a beginner-friendly grade. Though it's open to motorized vehicles, traffic is usually light to nonexistent, particularly during the week. From Helena, follow the directions to the mouth of Magpie Gulch in Ride 40 and park either at Jo Bonner Picnic Area on Canyon Ferry or at one of the pullouts along lower Magpie Road. From here you can do an up-and-back ride of any distance, from a few miles to nearly 30 miles if you pedal all the way to the Big Belt divide. True diehards can make a loop by climbing 15 miles to the divide then dropping down FR 359 into Avalanche Gulch. Run about 17 miles down yet another scenic cut in the Belts to Canyon Ferry Road (CR 284). Turn right and pedal about 5.5 miles north back to Magpie Gulch for a total of about 38 miles.

Confederate Gulch - This historic mining district is riddled with roads and doubletrack, a mountain biker's playground. Numerous interpretive signs recount the area's history, and rockhounds will enjoy panning for gold or hunting for mineral specimens and fossils among the mining debris. From Helena follow the access directions to Magpie Gulch in Ride 40. Continue south on Canyon Ferry Road (CR 284) another 13 miles to the signed left turn for Confederate Gulch (CR 287). Drive about 6 miles northwest to the heart of the mining district, a total of about 44 miles from Helena.

North and West Elkhorns

McClellan Creek - The terrain below Casey Peak in the northern Elkhorns looks inviting, but few bikers have yet ventured onto the trail network here. McClellan Creek Road probably offers the best access point to these easier trails. From Helena drive 4 miles south on Interstate 15 to Montana City. Exit and turn east on CR 518. Drive about 0.3 mile and turn right at the sign for McClellan Creek just before the

Montana City School. Go south through Saddle Mountain Estates almost 4 miles and take the left-hand fork (FR 294). Go another 2 miles and take the right-hand fork signed for Jackson Creek. Continue another 1.5 miles to the East Fork Trailhead, which is on the left just before a small bridge. Trail 343 goes east into the woods, and joins Trail 302 along the East Fork of McClellan Creek. Other trails branch north and south, offering multiple loop opportunities.

Tizer Lakes - Nearly every Helena mountain biker gets tempted into grunting up the rough and rollicking Prickly Pear Road (FR 424) to Tizer Lakes. Few people bother doing it more than once every couple of years. From Helena, drive about 12 miles south on I-15 to Jefferson City. Exit right and park in town by the Jefferson City Bar. Pedal back beneath the interstate and turn right onto the eastside frontage road going south. In just under 1 mile it turns east and begins climbing along Prickly Pear Creek. Cross the national forest boundary in another 4 miles and jam those pedals about 5 miles east on rugged jeep track, climbing hard most of the way. At a junction in a clearing atop a wide saddle on the Elkhorn divide, turn south, following signs for Tizer Lakes. The doubletrack gains another 1,000 feet in the next 3 miles to reach the lakes. Count on half a day for the 28-mile up-and-back round-trip.

Boulder Area

Muskrat and Rawhide Creeks - From Helena drive 29 miles south on I-15 to Boulder and turn north on the east side frontage road. Drive about 1.5 miles beside I-15 and turn east, going another 1.3 miles to a T-junction. Turn left, drive 1 mile north, and go right onto Muskrat Creek Road (FR 441). The road forks in about 1.4 miles—take the left branch for Muskrat Creek and Trail 72 or go right on Rawhide Creek Road to Trail 73. Either way, drive until you reach the national forest boundary and park well off the road. Now for the exploring . . . has anybody actually pedaled the length of these trails, either to the Tizer Lakes basin or over to Elkhorn?

Queen Gulch - Drive 29 miles south on I-15 to Boulder, then 7 miles south on MT 69. Turn left onto gravel Elkhorn Road (FR 258) and cross a bridge over the Boulder River. Turn right and drive east about 3 miles then turn left to stay on FR 258 going north toward the mountains. Drive another 7 miles and park at the mouth of Queen Gulch (it's signed for Queen Gulch and FR 8546).

There are three main options from here. **(1)** Pedal up Queen Gulch Road (FR 8546, then FR 8578) about 7 miles to the Elkhorn Skyline mine just below 9,432-foot Crow Peak. It's mostly moderate doubletrack through Douglas-fir and subalpine fir. Figure about 1.5 hours for the 14-mile round-trip. **(2)** Pedal about 3 miles up Queen Gulch (FR 8546), then turn right onto FR 8554 and climb to Radersburg Pass. Just over the pass, take the first right (FR 8579) and climb over the ridge to the south. The road then dips into the South Fork of Queen Gulch and wraps around an outlying knob before winding north to rejoin the Queen Gulch Road about 2.5 miles northeast of the start. The whole loop is about 13 miles; figure on 1.5 hours in the saddle. **(3)** Ride up Queen Gulch 3 miles and turn left onto a jeep track just past FR 9366 on the right. Roll over a low ridge and drop into the half-empty town of Elkhorn. Then bomb south on FR 258 about 2 miles to complete the loop at the mouth of Queen Gulch. This loop covers about 7 miles in an hour or less.

Farnham Gulch–Bull Mountain - From Helena drive 29 miles south on I-15 to Boulder. Continue another 2.5 miles south on MT 69 and turn right on the gravel road to Boulder Hot Springs. Drive about 200 yards and park at the Springs Hotel. Pedal west on the gravel road less than 1 mile, then go left (south) 1.3 miles on Whitetail Basin Road. About 0.4 mile past the national forest boundary sign look for a sandy jeep track (FR 8528) going left and uphill. Scamper up this mildly strenuous track to a three-way junction in another mile. Bear left on the northernmost two-track going east into the trees. In 0.4 mile the road crosses Farnham Creek and climbs into a pile of boulders. Beyond the rocks, a doubletrack threads among grassy clearings and aspen climbing south toward Bull Mountain. How far does it go? Perhaps all the way to Hadley Park and FR 8530 at the 7,000-foot level atop Bull Mountain. But most riders are content to turn around after 5 or 6 miles and roll back for a soak in Boulder Hot Springs. Set aside 1 hour for the up-and-back ride and at least 2 hours for the pools.

Galena Park Road - About 2 miles south of Boulder on Whitetail Basin Road, turn right onto the Little Boulder River Road (FR 86). In about 1 mile turn right onto the Galena Park Road (FR 638). This one-lane dirt road meanders northwest, climbing along a tributary stream to Galena Park in about 5.5 miles. From here, you can loop back on FR 8694 and FR 8582, or continue southwest on FR 8668 to explore a labyrinth of double- and singletrack routes (see the Deerlodge National Forest Travel Map).

Appendix B

Information Sources

Helena National Forest
2880 Skyway Drive
Helena, MT 59601
(406) 449-5201

Helena Ranger District
2001 Poplar
Helena, MT 59601
(406) 449-5490

Lincoln Ranger District
P.O. Box 219
Lincoln, MT 59639
(406) 362-4265

Townsend Ranger District
415 S. Front
Townsend, MT 59644
(406) 266-3425

U.S. Bureau of Land Management
Butte District Office
106 N. Parkmont
Butte, MT 59701
(406) 494-5059

U.S. Geological Survey
301 S. Park Avenue
Helena, MT 59601
(406) 441-1319

Montana Department of Fish, Wildlife and Parks
1420 East Sixth Avenue
Helena, MT 59620
(406) 444-2535

Open Space Helena
Box 653
Helena, MT 59624
(406) 449-1069

Prickly Pear Land Trust
P.O. Box 892
Helena, MT 59624
(406) 442-0490

City of Helena
Parks Administration
(406) 447-8463
Assesor's Office
(406) 442-6530

Bike Shops

Big Sky Cyclery
1419 11th Avenue
Helena City Plaza
Helena, MT 59601
(406) 442-4644

Capital Sports and Western
1092 Helena Avenue
Helena, MT 59601
(406) 443-2978

Great Divide Cyclery
336 N. Jackson
Helena, MT 59601
(406) 443-5188

Montana Outdoor Sports
708 N. Last Chance Gulch
Helena, MT 59601
(406) 443-4119

Glossary

ATB: All-terrain bicycle, a.k.a. mountain bike, sprocket rocket, fat-tire flyer.

ATV: All-terrain vehicle; in this book ATV refers to motorbikes and three- and four-wheelers designed for off-road use.

Bail: To get off the bike, usually in a hurry, whether or not you meant to. Often a last resort.

Bunny hop: Leaping up while riding, lifting both wheels off the ground to jump over an obstacle (or for sheer joy).

Clean: Riding without touching a foot (or other body part) to the ground; to ride a tough section successfully.

Clipless: A type of pedal with a binding that accepts a special cleat on the soles of bike shoes. The cleat clicks in for more control and efficient pedaling, and out for safe landings (in theory).

Contour: A line on a topographic map showing a continuous elevation level over uneven ground. Also used as a verb to indicate a fairly easy or moderate grade: "The trail contours around the west flank of the mountain before the final grunt to the top."

Dab: To put a foot or hand down (or hold onto or lean on a tree or other support) while riding. If you have to dab, then you haven't ridden that piece of trail **clean.**

Downfall: Trees that have fallen across the trail.

Doubletrack: A trail, jeep road, ATV route, or other track with two distinct ribbons of **tread,** typically with grass growing in between. No matter which side you choose, the other rut always looks smoother.

Endo: Lifting the rear wheel off the ground and riding (or abruptly not riding) on the front wheel only. Also known, at various degrees, as a nose wheelie, "going over the handlebars," and a face plant.

Fall line: The angle and direction of a slope; the **line** you follow when gravity is in control and you aren't.

Graded: When a gravel road is scraped level to smooth out the washboards and potholes, it has been *graded*. In this book, a road is listed as graded only if it is regularly maintained. Not all such roads are graded every year, however.

Granny gear: The innermost and smallest of the three chainrings on the bottom bracket spindle (where the pedals and crank arms attach to the bike's frame). Shift down to your granny gear (and up to the biggest cog on the rear hub) to find your lowest (easiest) gear for climbing.

Hammer: To ride hard; derived from how it feels afterward—"I'm hammered."

Hammerhead: Someone who actually enjoys feeling **hammered.** A Type A personality rider who goes hard and fast all the time.

Kelly hump: An abrupt mound of dirt across the road or trail. These are common on old logging roads and skidder tracks, placed there to block vehicle access. At high speeds, they become launching pads for bikes and inadvertent astronauts.

Line: The route (or trajectory) between or over obstacles or through turns. **Tread** or trail refers to the ground you're riding on; the line is the path you choose within the tread (and exists mostly in the eye of the beholder).

Off-the-seat: Moving your butt behind the bike seat and over the rear tire; it's a move used for control on extremely steep descents. This position increases braking power, helps prevent **endos,** and reduces skidding.

Portage: To carry the bike, usually up a steep hill, across unrideable obstacles, or through a stream.

Quads: Thigh muscles (short for quadraceps) or maps in the USGS topographic series (short for quadrangles). Nice quads of either kind can help get you out of trouble in the backcountry.

Ratcheting: Pedaling backwards to avoid hitting rocks or other obstacles with the pedals, a.k.a. backpedaling.

Sidehill: Where the trail crosses a slope. If the **tread** is narrow, keep your inside (uphill) pedal up to avoid hitting the ground. If the tread tilts downhill, you may have to use some body language to keep the bike plumb (vertical) to avoid slipping out.

Singletrack: A trail, game run, or other track with only one ribbon of **tread**—but this is like defining an orgasm as a muscle cramp. Good singletrack is pure fun.

Spur: A side road or trail that splits off from the main route.

Surf: Riding through loose gravel or sand that lets wheels sway from side to side. Also *heavy surf:* frequent and difficult obstacles.

Suspension: A bike with front suspension has a shock-absorbing fork or stem. Rear suspension absorbs shock between the rear wheel and frame. A bike with both is said to be fully suspended.

Switchbacks: When a trail goes up a steep slope, it zigzags or *switchbacks* across the **fall line** to ease the gradient of the climb. Well-designed switchbacks make a turn with at least an 8-foot radius and remain fairly level within the turn itself. These are rare, however, and cyclists often struggle to ride through sharply angled, sloping switchbacks.

Track stand: Balancing on a bike in one place, without rolling forward appreciably; to do so, cock the front wheel to one side and bring that pedal up to the 1 or 2 o'clock position. Now control your side-to-side balance by applying pressure on the pedals and brakes and changing the angle of the front wheel, as needed. It takes practice but really comes in handy at stoplights, on **switchbacks,** and when trying to free a foot before falling.

Tread: The riding surface, particularly regarding **singletrack.**

Water bar: A log, rock, or other barrier placed in the **tread** to divert water off the trail and prevent erosion. Peeled logs can be slippery and cause bad falls, especially when they angle sharply across the trail.

A Short Index of Rides

Road Rides (includes jeep tracks and unmaintained routes)

Sweet Singletrack Rides (may also include road and doubletrack portions)

Beginner's Luck

Technical Tests

Great Climbs—The Yearn to Burn

Great Downhills—The Need for Speed

About the Author

Will Harmon traces his love for the outdoors back to a childhood spent rummaging through the undergrowth of a 140-acre hardwood forest in southeastern Pennsylvania. More recently (disguised as an adult), he earned a Bachelor of Arts in English from the University of Montana and has enjoyed working as a backpacking, skiing, and rafting guide; wilderness ranger and trail builder for the USDA Forest Service; and writer specializing in nature, outdoor recreation, and natural resource management. He is the author of *The Hiker's Guide to Alberta* and numerous educational articles and handbooks. Will lives in Helena, Montana, with his wife Rose and their two sons, Evan and Ben.

get
FALCON GUIDED

FALCON GUIDES® are available for where-to-go hiking, mountain biking, rock climbing, walking, scenic driving, fishing, rockhounding, paddling, birding, wildlife viewing, and camping. We also have FalconGuides on essential outdoor skills and subjects and field identification. The following titles are currently available, but this list grows every year. For a free catalog with a complete list of titles, call FALCON toll-free at 1-800-582-2665.

MOUNTAIN BIKING GUIDES

Mountain Biking Arizona
Mountain Biking Colorado
Mountain Biking New Mexico
Mountain Biking New York
Mountain Biking Northern New England
Mountain Biking Southern New England
Mountain Biking Utah

LOCAL CYCLING SERIES

Fat Trax Bozeman
Fat Trax Colorado Springs
Mountain Biking Bend
Mountain Biking Boise
Mountain Biking Chequamegon
Mountain Biking Denver/Boulder
Mountain Biking Durango
Mountain Biking Helena
Mountain Biking Moab

■ *To order any of these books, check with your local bookseller or call FALCON ® at*
1-800-582-2665.

Visit us on the world wide web at:
www.falconguide.com

FALCON®